CORONATION STREET
1960~ STREET ~1985
25 Years

Edited by Graham Nown

CBC Enterprises
Montréal · Toronto · New York · London

Published by CBC Enterprises, a division of the Canadian
Broadcasting Corporation, Box 500, Station A, Toronto
(Ontario), Canada M5W 1E6.

First published in Great Britain in 1985 by Ward Lock
Limited, 82 Gower Street, London WC1E 6EQ.
An Egmont Company.

Canadian Cataloguing in Publication Data

Main entry under title:
Coronation Street : 25 years
ISBN 0-88794-231-8

1. Coronation Street (Television program) –
History. I. CBC Enterprises.
PN1992.77.C67C6 1985 791.45'72 C85-099315-6

Printed and bound in Italy

Distributed to the trade by McClelland and Stewart
Limited, Toronto

Contents

SILVER JUBILEE CELEBRATION 9

CORONATION STREET BEHIND THE SCENES 17

WHAT THE PAPERS SAW 21

THE MAN WHO INVENTED CORONATION STREET 24

ON AND OFF THE STREET 27

A CORONATION STREET WHO'S WHO 30

HOW CORONATION STREET WAS BORN 67

HALF AN HOUR OF TELEVISION HISTORY – THE FIRST
  EPISODE 70

A WALK ROUND WEATHERFIELD 92

CORONATION STREET – THE NEXT TWENTY-FIVE YEARS 94

ON THE STREET WHERE THEY LIVE . . . 97

TWENTY-FIVE YEARS: A CORONATION STREET DIARY 101

TWENTY-FIVE THINGS YOU NEVER KNEW ABOUT
  CORONATION STREET 201

THE STREET'S FORGOTTEN STARS 203

JUST HOW STREET-WISE ARE YOU? 210

Grateful thanks to Granada Television, and the cast and production team of Britain's greatest television programme. Especially to *Coronation Street* Executive Producer Bill Podmore for his help and endless enthusiasm, the amazing memory of Eric Rosser, the Street's official archivist, and the untiring efforts of Joan Riley and Leita Donn of Granada Press Office.

'Manchester produces what to me is the Pickwick Papers. That is to say, *Coronation Street*. Mondays and Wednesdays, I live for them. Thank God, half past seven tonight and I shall be in paradise . . .'

SIR JOHN BETJEMAN

Silver Jubilee celebration

As Russell Harty once said: 'There was life before *Coronation Street*. But it didn't add up to much . . .' The Street is no longer just a television programme. It has become a part of British life, making it hard to imagine what things would be like without it. And by setting the highest standards of drama and production, twice a week for twenty five years, it has changed the face of television.

Praise has been lavished upon it from Buckingham Palace, 10 Downing Street, the Royal Television Society . . . the feathers in its Northern flat cap are countless. Even the critics have eaten their words. The *Daily Mirror*'s Ken Irwin predicted after the first episode in 1960: 'The programme is doomed from the outset – with its signature tune and grim scene of a row of terraced houses and smoking chimneys . . .' Twenty years later he wrote: 'What can I say but congratulations all round. Best wishes on your 2000th episode.'

Coronation Street was first screened on 9 December 1960. By midsummer the following year it had made such an impact that Blackpool Corporation asked the cast to switch on their £500,000 illuminations. Previous celebrities invited to perform the task had included Jayne Mansfield, the Russian and American Ambassadors, and international footballer Stanley Matthews.

It has become the world's longest-running television series, attracting millions of fans from Salford to Singapore. Over the years it has been seen on all five continents. No matter where the viewers are, there are Barlows and Tilsleys and Duckworths on the street where they live. They may eat rice or ride in a Rolls, but the life and laughter of the Street is a common currency: Hilda's beady-eyed battle to scale life's peaks; Annie Walker's Herculean efforts to bring a touch of class to the Rovers Return; Ken Barlow's restless aspirations; the military precision of Percy Sugden; wilting Mavis waiting for Mr Wonderful; Mike Baldwin, the tough boss with the soft centre; and Bet Lynch, well, what more can be said about that subtle dress sense? Life in a terraced street in the north of England can be translated into any language.

Coronation Street's appeal appears to know no age or social barriers. Schoolchildren are often given homework tasks based on the Street. Others research *Coronation Street* 'projects', and

1963 brought the first of many awards for the best TV show in Britain.

Famous faces – the cast take a break in 1969.

sometimes whole classes are told to write letters to their favourite Street characters. Schoolboys at Eton contacted the studio asking for *Coronation Street* scripts. 'We watch it during the holidays, but we have no TV at school,' they explained.

When the Government Information Service wanted an excerpt from a typical British television programme to send to overseas stations, they did not have to think twice – it was *Coronation Street*. Or, as the *Daily Express* chose to put it: 'With all those opinion polls telling us how Britain is changing out of sight, the wonderful world of the Street is the only reality

we've got to cling to. The Street survives while Britain becomes a bad soap opera.'

When Britain converted to decimal currency, there seemed no better idea to 'sell' it to the nation than to use the new fifty pence piece in the programme. An official from the Royal Mint brought one of the first strikings of the new coin to the studio. He waited until the scene was in the can, took his coin back, and returned to London.

Great care is taken by producers and writers, backed by the formidable archives of *Coronation Street* historian Eric Rosser, to ensure that everything is right. Street viewers have long memories and reach for a pen or telephone at the tiniest inconsistency. Eagle-eyed enthusiasts notice even the smallest details of the sets and props. When one of Hilda Ogden's plaster ducks slipped on her living room wall, Terry Wogan's morning radio show was swamped with letters.

A darts enthusiast pointed out in the early days of the programme that the wrong kind of darts board was in the Rovers, so the design department swiftly changed it. Another viewer noticed that an out-of-date boxing poster was still on the wall of the pub. It was explained away as a souvenir of the time a local boy had his first fight at Manchester's Free Trade Hall.

Some viewers, believe it or not, ask where they can buy the furniture they see in *Coronation Street*, or where they can get the pictures they see on the walls. Van Gogh prints sold well when one hung over Frank Barlow's mantelpiece in the early years. And when Hilda had her first mural – or, as she called it, her 'muriel' – requests poured in from viewers asking where they could buy an Alpine scene like it.

Many go further and regard the scripted activities of the *Coronation Street* cast as real-life happenings. At Christmas they try to book the Rovers Return for parties. Whenever a terraced house becomes vacant, they write in asking if they can rent it. When Hilda went off for a few week's holiday a lady wrote offering to take over her cleaning job at the Rovers. A Midlands marriage bureau staff were so worried about Bet Lynch's future that they offered to go through their books to find an eligible man. And those outrageous earrings, incidentally, arrive by the boxful. One little five-year-old girl sent a large pair of green plastic discs. She said they were her favourite earrings when she played at dressing up, and she always got more boyfriends when she wore them. She was sending them to Bet so that she could get more boyfriends too.

A cake for the Street's eighteenth birthday in 1978.

The fans keep dropping in – from Howard Keel to cub-scouts, parties of pensioners, and from Dustin Hoffman to Diana Dors.

There are times when it seems that half the world is waiting in the wings ready to give advice, or solve the Street's entirely fictional problems. When Elsie Tanner was knocked down by a London taxi, and unable to be identified, her screen husband received an avalanche of mail telling him that she had not come home because she was lying ill in hospital. And when the Street's Over-Sixties Club struggled to raise money for a new piano, people rang the studios offering their own. Scores of girls wrote for a job at the Rovers when a barmaid left, and a lady whose window cleaner had let her down dropped a line to Stan Ogden asking if he could take over. Good tradesmen, they say, are hard to find – which perhaps explains why the same lady has not written to Jack Duckworth.

But even the Street cannot keep everyone happy . . . one viewer complained that wallpaper used on one set was exactly the same as his own living room wallpaper – and to make it worse, Granada had hung it upside down. But few can compete with the viewer who went to a ball in a gown she had painstakingly made herself from fabric bought at a local drapers. When she swept in with her husband, who was resplendent in dinner jacket and black tie, a friend whispered to her: 'Do you know that your dress is made from the same material as the curtains in the Rovers Return?' Annie Walker would have been immensely impressed.

Everyone who works on *Coronation Street* displays a great affection for the programme. And therein, perhaps, lies a secret of its success. Hollywood director Michael Apted directed episode 668, back in May 1967, in which the train ploughed over the Viaduct at the end of the Street. '*Coronation Street* was the very first programme I directed,' he recalls. 'It was where I really learned about actors and scripts. You had to deal with every kind of actor – those who were already stars in their own right, and those who were as new to the business as I was. They were all extremely kind to me. It was tough going for them, but they never seemed to be thrown. They were unstintingly helpful and generous.'

Mike Scott, now Granada's Programme Controller, directed several of the early episodes, including the gas mains emergency evacuation story in episode sixteen when all the Street folk were unwillingly bundled into the Glad Tidings Mission Hall for the night. 'It is fortunate that nobody took much notice of my first response to *Coronation Street*,' he says. 'As a young director I was asked to read scripts, and opined that it would do well in the north-west of England, but

The cast celebrate the Street's Twenty-first Anniversary.

The original four – Ken, Elsie, Albert and Annie – toast twenty-one years of *Coronation Street*.

that it would never succeed in the rest of Great Britain. How wrong can you be! Twenty-five years later it is amazing to realize that the show is not only alive and well, but of such a consistently high standard.'

Coronation Street's Dickensian characters inspired scriptwriter Geoffrey Lancashire to write many other plays and serial episodes for television. His first TV script was for *Coronation Street*, and since then he has written countless episodes, including Elsie Tanner's memorable wedding. 'I firmly believe,' he says, 'that the rich diversity of characters in the Street, which range from the teenager to the pensioner, the good to the gossipy, the vacuous and the crotchety, the pretentious and the academic, the doting and the dotty, helped me later to write all forms of television drama.'

It is surprising just how far the homely appeal of *Coronation Street* has spread in twenty-five years. When the Street reached its two thousandth episode, Prime Minister Margaret Thatcher telegrammed: 'There must be few people in Britain who have not heard of the Rovers Return,

or become involved in the lives of Ena Sharples, Albert Tatlock, Annie Walker, Elsie Tanner and Ken Barlow . . . To have sustained such popularity is a tremendous achievement . . . Long may your success continue.' At least two other Prime Ministers have been self-declared Street fans. James Callaghan claimed to be a devoted follower, and Sir Harold Wilson's Cabinet meetings on Mondays and Wednesdays are reported to have seldom extended beyond 7.30 p.m.

Russell Harty, Michael Parkinson and Willis Hall went so far as to launch the British League for Hilda Ogden, and persuaded arch-fan Sir John Betjeman to become Honorary Life President. Others who have publicly declared their affection for the Street include Lord Olivier (who once expressed a wish to make a guest appearance opposite Annie Walker), the late Diana Dors, Roy Orbison and Ella Fitzgerald.

Coronation Street is, of course, as British as warm beer, but its popularity has reached parts that other TV series haven't. On the Hawaiian island of Oahu, where they filmed *Magnum* and

Hawaii Five-O, the local choice was *Coronation Street*. Fans tuned in on the beach at dusk with their portable TVs beneath tropical palms. In Zambia, where you have to be mad to wear a cloth cap, it was streets ahead. Scandinavians mercifully had subtitles to relieve the anxiety of struggling with such northernisms as 'hey up!' and 'by 'eck!' And thanks to a new transmitter, the Falklands have joined the world-wide network of connoisseurs of Corner Shop gossip and the goings-on at the Rovers Return.

Once *Coronation Street* breaks a record it has a habit of breaking it repeatedly. In November 1984, for instance, the programme achieved the highest audience figure for television drama in two and a half years, with 20.45 million viewers. By January 1985 it had broken that record no fewer than four times, winning a highest-ever audience of 21.4 millions. Since 1981 the only programmes to have beaten it were the James Bond films and the movie *Jaws*.

Among the international army of devotees are viewers in Canada, where the Street is screened every day with an omnibus edition on Sundays. Granada TV, in what was the biggest sale ever made to a television network, sold seven years of *Coronation Street* episodes to CBC – 728 programmes beamed to big cities as well as remote communities in snow-bound Goose Bay and Labrador. Forty-two stations broadcasting to Canada's sixteen million English-speaking people screened the Street.

Two years later CBC bought another 208 episodes. At about the same time, Producer Bill Podmore, Julie Goodyear (Bet Lynch), Johnny Briggs (Mike Baldwin), and Christopher Quinten (Brian Tilsley) flew to Toronto. Julie proved a huge attraction, and TV stations were innundated with requests for her photograph. On CBC's local Toronto station the switchboard was completely jammed by fans responding to a *Coronation Street* phone-in. When the Street's old outdoor set was demolished, 100 souvenir bricks were flown out by Air Canada to be sold at a charity auction to the highest bidders. Jean Alexander (Hilda Ogden) and Geoff Hughes (Eddie Yeats) attended the dinner and auctioned the original Rovers Return sign. The Street made the *Guinness Book of Records* in 1971 when a Canadian TV station, Saskatoon, bought 1,142 episodes – the biggest-ever single sale of a television programme.

When Swedish Television decided to launch its own twice-weekly drama series, two of the production team spent a week in Manchester learning from the experts. Their verdict: 'It was an entertaining and instructional visit. We were particularly impressed by the professionalism of the actors, and also by the warm atmosphere and family spirit of the entire team.'

In 1984 Gibraltar Television decided its viewers could not live without the Street and began transmitting episodes, making a total of eighteen countries around the world to receive regular reports of life in Weatherfield. In New Zealand and Australia the programme was consistently among the most successful television series screened. The Dutch television station VARA bought fifty-two episodes in 1984, but viewers in Holland are still following the events of 1982 when Deirdre Barlow came close to wrecking her marriage to dull, dependable Ken.

One of the Street's earliest overseas forays was in 1966 when Pat Phoenix (Elsie Tanner), Arthur Leslie (Jack Walker) and Doris Speed (Annie Walker) flew to Australia after a send-off at No. 10 (Downing, not Coronation, Street!) from Harold Wilson. They plunged into a hectic round of chat-shows and public appearances. At Melbourne hundreds of flag-waving fans waited at the airport to watch their motorcade . . . They would never have believed it back in Rosamund Street.

Coronation Street won fans across America when it was transmitted daily on the USA Cable Network in 1982 to a potential audience of ten million. Six months later they were asking for more, and ordered another 130 episodes. Fan mail which arrives at the *Coronation Street* office from all over the world began to include postmarks from New York: 'A sheer delight!' was typical of hundreds received. St Louis, Missouri, summed it up with: 'We are completely hooked on it.' And desperate fans in Kennebunk, Maine, pleaded: 'Don't stop now! Please continue until we are current with the series shown in England – and then *keep going!*'

Perhaps the greatest accolade, and proudest moment for everyone concerned with *Coronation Street*, came when the Queen and Prince Philip toured the newly-built outdoor set in 1982. Surrounded by an eight-foot wall behind Granada's central Manchester studios, it is a long-lasting, life-size momument to Britain's greatest television series. And to satisfy those eagle-eyed viewers, no detail was overlooked. 'Dennis Tanner 1951' was carved into a faded window-frame – and one vital architectural change was made to satisfy the handful who had

The Queen and Prince Philip
visit the Street.

Doris Speed lays the foundation stone for the new outdoor lot.

The new Street takes shape.

been puzzled by *Coronation Street*'s oldest mystery. The door to the Gents in the Rovers Return had always given the unmistakable impression of leading into Albert Tatlock's kitchen. As someone shrewdly observed 'Maybe that's why he's always so grumpy.' To avoid further confusion, a tiny passageway was built between Albert's and the pub.

To give the Street set its faded, authentic look, it was built flanking a real cobbled street which is still visible in the derelict railway marshalling yard. Experts from the Building Design Partnership toured demolition sites, and returned with 49,000 old bricks from terraced Salford streets and 6,500 reclaimed roofing slates. They were strengthened by hidden concrete blocks, and

knitted with mortar mixed with paint to give the brickwork a pre-war drabness. The finished lot, with Baldwin's Casuals, the Viaduct and a section of Rosamund Street, was a tremendous improvement on the old indoor set which had stood for twenty years. And, of course, there was the added realism of Manchester's pudding-bag clouds floating low overhead. Weatherfield had finally come to life.

The Queen, fascinated by the achievement, was interested to know exactly where Coronation Street was supposed to be situated. With only a trace of a smile, a studio executive replied: 'In the hearts and minds of your people, Ma'am.'

And all of us would raise a glass of Newton and Ridley's to that . . .

Coronation Street behind the scenes

Bill Podmore, *Coronation Street*'s Executive Producer, has been associated with the world's longest-running TV series for almost a decade . . .

My first association with *Coronation Street* was way back in 1964 as a senior cameraman. I had travelled up with my crew from London to help out in the Manchester studios on the coverage of the General Election. The programme and the characters had by this time become household names, although most of my young 'bloods' didn't know Ena Sharples from Albert Tatlock.

Bill Podmore.

They were sorted out in double-quick time when one of them asked which one was Ena. Just one glower under the famous hair net had them shaking in their suede shoes.

Some seven years later, as a newly-trained programme director, I was scheduled to direct my first two episodes of *Coronation Street*. To say I was nervous would be an understatement – I was terrified. Terrified at the thought of telling these famous and well-established artists what to do. Yet again it was Ena Sharples who, as I walked through the rehearsal room doors, put it all into

perspective with the greeting: 'Hello Bill, welcome. My train leaves at 5.30.' Then she smiled: I laughed and all was well. They were, as now, a great team of professionals determined to do their best in the short time there is in which to rehearse and record two episodes per week.

I subsequently moved on to producing and directing many comedy series until December 1975 when I was, as we say, 'called upstairs' to be asked how I felt about producing *Coronation Street*. I remember trying to say something, but my mouth would not move. It was totally unexpected. And, believe me, the thought of being responsible for producing not only the longest-running but also the most successful drama series ever, was a very daunting one. After swallowing deeply a couple of times, my mouth opened and I heard myself saying I would give it a go for a year. Here I am, nine years later, still happily involved in the series.

I often think of a remark someone made after being persuaded to produce yet another series of *Dr Who*: 'It is the only prison I know where you get time *on* for good behaviour.'

Taking over such an established programme means one inherits not only the now-legendary largest desk in the world, but a successful production system which has evolved from years of experience. This all basically revolves around a three week turn-round. Every third Monday the Story Conference is held, attended by all the current writers – ten at present – the two storyline writers, a historian, secretary and producer. The agenda, which is prepared the previous week, consists of any on-going stories plus suggestions and requests for story ideas, particularly involving characters who have not recently been featured.

The object of these, often heated, meetings is to provide outlines for six episodes which, of course, cover three weeks' transmission. The two storyline writers first chart these six episodes, and we go through, in some detail, the development of the stories under discussion. In any one episode it is necessary to have at least two stories, and we

17

Bill and his *Coronation Street* 'family'.

try to achieve a balance of drama and comedy when considering them. There are, of course, exceptions – for instance, if one episode is highly dramatic, it might well be indelicate to have a comedy story running alongside.

Where do all the stories come from as, after twenty-five years, it seems they all must have been used more than once? Maybe some of them have! The programme consumes stories with the appetite of a whale, and it is a most difficult task for everyone concerned to generate new and fresh ideas that are going to keep the characters satisfied, and the Street popular.

The stories mulled over at the meeting are about three months ahead of transmission. Storyline writers then have two weeks in which to prepare detailed synopses of these episodes, presented in a scene-by-scene breakdown. As they are writing they also have to keep in mind members of the cast who are not directly involved, but who will be used in various common areas of the Street to help colour and advance the stories.

While they are working, the writers who have been commissioned from the previous conference will be delivering their scripts. In the third week these are read by the producer and the storyline writers to check for continuity. The three pairs of finished scripts are then handed over to the appropriate director.

By Monday morning of the third week the producer is generally commissioning six writers to work on each of the next six programmes. There are occasions when, because of the content, it is an advantage to have one writer working on a pair of scripts. This, however, is unusual as it places great demands on their time. On the Thursday we have a Commissioning Conference

Ena and Elsie relax between takes.

which the writers attend – a lively meeting when we discuss the continuity of the storylines, and how to establish any new characters. Each writer criticizes the way the storylines have been produced and, after discussion, they may be altered to improve the programme. The writers then have two weeks to go away and labour on their episodes.

At any one time there are three directors working on the programme – the first collecting his scripts, his colleague in the second week of preparation, and the third who is busy with rehearsals and recording.

When a director receives his scripts his first job is to study them and discuss any problems with the designer. Then, with the Outside Broadcast planner, he talks over any outdoor filming, especially if it happens to be beyond the Street's external set. He also discusses with the casting department, and the producer, any extra parts that may have been written into the script. It is the director's task to prepare a camera script – a detailed visual interpretation which breaks down into something like 200 separate shots distributed among three cameras.

Any outside filming is done first, on Monday morning, and is usually complete in time for afternoon rehearsals at 2 p.m. In the rehearsal room the outlines of the walls of the sets are marked out on the floor with plastic tape and the furniture improvised. As the afternoon goes on, the director plots each scene, working out where the cast will be standing, or moving to, or entering from. These are the pure mechanics of the Street, but they are very critical because the director, up to now, has only visualized them in his camera script. The more precisely the artists

Monday morning filming on the new lot.

are placed, the more accurately they remember their positions – making it easier for the cameramen to obtain their shots, and helping everyone gain a march on our biggest enemy, time.

Before rehearsals finish, around 5.30 p.m., the cast will have been asked by the make-up and wardrobe department what their requirements for the two episodes are.

Tuesday rehearsals, when everyone has a better knowledge of their positions, tend to concentrate on the interpretation of the scripts. They run from 10.30 a.m. until about 5.30 in the evening, and give the actors an opportunity to talk to the director and producer if they think the dialogue could be better changed to suit their character.

Rehearsals on Wednesdays continue until lunchtime, and then at 2.15 p.m. we have what is known as a 'technical run'. This is when the lighting director arrives at the rehearsal room to note the artists' positions in each set, and draw up his lighting plan. It is also the first opportunity for the producer to properly assess the artistic interpretation of each episode. While all this is happening, the technical supervisor evaluates the situation, the senior cameraman draws the director's attention to any problems he sees, the sound supervisor makes his checks, and the production assistant times each episode to ensure it lasts exactly 24 minutes and 30 seconds.

Out of all this *Coronation Street* is slowly taking shape – technical problems are ironed-out, the producer passes any notes he has made to the director, and the writer – if he is available – will also be there, closely guarding the lines he has sweated over.

The old outdoor set is demolished.

On Wednesday night, when everyone has gone, the sets are hauled into the studio and dressed with their furnishings, ready for Thursday morning when the lighting director moves in with his electricians. The lighting has to be completed by 1 p.m. and, together with the size of the studio, imposes a limit of five sets in any one episode.

During the next ninety minutes the designer and prop men take over, making adjustments, and ensuring that all the props are in exactly the correct positions – right down to that tilted plaster duck on Hilda Ogden's living room wall. By 2.30 p.m. everything is ready for the cameras and sound equipment, and rehearsals and recordings start. Each scene is rehearsed until everyone is happy, and then it is recorded on videotape. More often than not, the scenes are recorded out of sequence in an order determined by the director during the planning stages.

On the final day, Friday, a similar studio schedule runs from 9.30 a.m. until 6.30 in the evening. After the weekend the director and his production assistant disappear into the editing suite and have about three and a half hours in which to edit the completed programmes, for transmission the following week. On the same day he collects his next two scripts!

From all this hectic precision *Coronation Street* emerges – some weeks, I think, only by a miracle! A multitude of problems present themselves to the producer. Apart from adopting, as it were, a *Coronation Street* family and all their related problems, one also has a responsibility to millions of viewers who are constantly phoning and writing with criticism, praise, requests. 'Is Elsie's house still for sale, as I am very interested?' 'Are there any jobs going in Baldwin's factory? We are good workers and won't let him down.' Can I be this, that and the other in Coronation Street? What you need in the Rovers is . . . Wouldn't it be a good idea if . . .

Various organizations, charities and socially responsible organizations write asking if it might be possible to portray their respective causes in some way or other. It is all a great compliment to the writers, artists and production team that the programme is held in such esteem. *Coronation Street*'s reflection of life is so credible that it is considered to be real, and its powerful scenario draws attention in a very real way to the problems existing in our society.

On 9 December 1985 we celebrate the Silver Anniversary of the programme. I don't imagine I'll be around for the Golden – but I am sure the programme will!

What the papers saw

Coronation Street attracts world-wide interest, occupying columns of newsprint every day. In addition to letters from fans, comment from the critics, and journalists looking for a story, cartoonists love to take a tongue-in-cheek look at Britain's most successful TV programme . . .

I *know* they're a couple of wallies, Mavis, but you've got to pretend to like one of them.

I think she just got back from Barbados or something...

Forget the script – just keep talking about your private lives.

It's not going to change his life, he says, but if you're buying a drink his is champagne.

Well, Deirdre, my advice is stick with Ken Barlow and introduce *me* to
Mike Baldwin.

"Granada's brought in Windsor Davis to smarten 'em up!"

The man who invented Coronation Street

Tony Warren created the story of everyday life in Weatherfield, along with some of the Street's most famous characters. But even he had no idea just how successful it would become . . .

One day in 1958 I walked into the Granada building in Manchester as an unemployed actor, and emerged two hours later as a writer. I was twenty-two years old and it was almost as simple as that. *Coronation Street* was certainly the end result.

I was a former boy actor who had out-grown his talent by getting tall. The casting director I called upon at Granada was Margaret Morris. A woman of rare perception, she could get those people who were not afraid of her to talk. She discovered that I was already writing for fun, and that fun was beginning to turn into money. She showed little interest in my acting ability, merely commenting that I was at an awkward age. Instead, she grilled me as to just what I had been

writing. She then picked up a telephone and set up a meeting which was to change my life.

It was with Harry Elton, a huge Canadian television producer, whose brief at Granada was to find talent. People either loved Harry Elton or ran a mile. He never seemed to stop talking. A lot of this might have been hot air, but some was purest gold. He could also listen when he felt the occasion demanded it. Without Harry Elton, *Coronation Street* would never have seen the light of day.

Almost immediately he commissioned me to write some episodes of a detective serial called Shadow Squad. Within six months he found me a job on the Granada staff in the Promotions Department, where we made trailers and wrote

Tony Warren.

scripts for the announcers. Within a year I was under exclusive contract to the company as a writer. This was considered something of an experiment. I was to have twelve months' financial security; Granada Television would automatically own everything I wrote, edited, altered or adapted during that period. The experiment can be said to have paid off, because this is how they acquired *Coronation Street*.

Newspaper articles have frequently tried to suggest that I am somehow bitter about this, but it is not the case. I am one of the happiest people I know. I would have been very bad at being a millionaire.

Much of this contractual period was spent attempting to turn Captain W.E. Johns' *Biggles* adventures into television episodes. Other writers could do this with ease, but I was hopeless at it. I begged to be allowed to write about something I knew and understood. I knew about the theatre and the north of England. Looking out through his office window, across the canal, at the great black panorama of Salford, Elton said: 'What about the story of a street out there?'

The same idea had already occurred to me. Eighteen months previously I had submitted to the BBC a pilot script for a series entitled 'Our Street'. To this day I await their reactions. All I ever received at the time was a bare acknowledgement that it had arrived safely. The chances are the script I sent to them was very raw, but the basics were certainly there.

The script Harry Elton urged me to create was written overnight on a burst of thrilled energy. With a few additions which I made later, this was to be precisely the script transmitted as episode one on Friday, 9 December 1960, at 7 p.m. But I am going too quickly. For a while it looked as though the show would never get off the ground.

Originally it had the working title of 'Florizel Street'. I had reasoned that the street name had either to be so familiar that every town had one, or romantic enough to be memorable. The theory was right, but Florizel was wrong. Harry and I were working under a cloak of near-secrecy. He urged me on to write episodes two and three, and the girls in the typing pool became our first fans. All along the pre-production way people seemed to *recognize* the show and take it to their hearts. Four episodes were eventually completed to sell the idea, within the company, to the Granada powers-that-be. Harry got this work out of me in record time, and then demanded an explanatory memorandum.

How to explain the new programme in one small memo? It took me nearly as long to think it out as it did to write a whole episode: 'A fascinating freemasonry, a volume of unwritten rules. These are the driving forces behind life in a working class street in the north of England. The purpose of "Florizel Street" is to examine a community of this nature, and to entertain.' Harry Elton went upstairs to do the selling job, armed with his own arguments and primed with some of mine.

Granada had the Independent Television licence to transmit in an area covering the greater part of the north of England. They had a firm commitment to reflect life in that area. It could, at the time, have been argued that the shows they were transmitting barely met this obligation. A point in our favour.

Granada had said they would bring employment to the region and they had – for production and administrative staff. Their leading actors were imported from London. Northern actors frequently had ineradicable northern accents, and these were unfashionable. For the most part they were only used in very small roles and in crowd scenes. I knew from having worked as an actor in radio and the theatre with these people, that we were sitting on a gold mine. Not only could we reflect the region, we could make the very accent fashionable.

The working class revolution was already on in the theatre, and just creeping into the cinema. I think we can be said to have played our part in bringing it to television. All that seems nothing now but at the time, believe me, the very idea was heady stuff indeed. It had not escaped our notice that the chairman of Granada, Sidney Bernstein, was a committed socialist. In the event it was his brother Cecil who pledged active support, and allowed us to attempt to make two experimental episodes. In case these succeeded I was to go on writing up to episode twelve, and to plan a possible bulldozing of the Street for what might prove to be a final thirteenth episode.

It was at this point that we expanded into a complete production team. Harry Elton remained as Executive Producer and Stuart Latham became Producer. The latter came from the south of England, and brought in a northern writer. H.V. Kershaw, to be what Latham described as 'a sounding board'. We did not clash and Harry Kershaw was very helpful as I struggled with some of the early storylines. Harry has always maintained that my strength as a writer lies in drawing characters and writing credible dialogue. When the writing team was formed he became a founder member, and went on to have a whole variety of production credits at the end of *Coronation Street* episodes. The *eventual* clash between us was inevitable. He openly regarded me as mercurial and disruptive. I have made no secret of the fact that I found him cautious – a man who was always careful to cover his bets. I am almost certainly describing both our professional strengths; today we have considerable respect for one another.

The designer assigned to the project was Dennis Parkin, and he and I toured Salford looking for a street which would match up with what I had written. We settled on Archie Street in the Ordsall district. With some minor adaptations it was used for opening title shots and a small quantity of early open-air location work. From his first sight of the first script Dennis Parkin believed passionately in the show, as did Derek Bennett, who directed episode one.

Auditions began – we saw hundreds of actors and actresses and assembled a trial cast. Margaret Morris was the Casting Director, but she listened hard to her assistant Jose Scott. Jose had been an actress in northern repertory companies, and these proved to be our main source of talent.

These early episodes were only made to show the potential to the men upstairs. It is interesting to note that Mike Scott, who directed the second, has today become a man upstairs himself. In 1960 some of them failed to see the potential in 'Florizel Street'. A rumour came down that one of them had said: 'The advertisers will withdraw their advertising.'

Harry Elton refused to be beaten. He ordered television sets to be mounted strategically around the Granada complex, and invited everyone who worked there to a public showing. Having seen the programme, they were invited to complete a questionnaire. The response was vivid, and in many ways indicative of what was to come from the general public. Some people firmly disliked it, but for every detractor there were ten others whose enthusiasm ranged from warm to ecstatic.

We were back in business, but I was asked seriously to consider deleting the role of Ena Sharples. Countless camera tests had failed to throw up an actress of sufficient age who had the cruel vitality the part demanded. A new species of star quality was called for. I refused to cut the part, and I was told that unless I could come up with a solution, I would simply have to think again. An actress who had smacked my bottom when I was a small boy on radio *Children's Hour* sprang to mind – Violet Carson. As far as I was concerned that was the last difficult piece of the jigsaw in place.

Anyone who was working at Granada Television on Friday, 9 December 1960, remembers it with affectionate awe. The sort of night legends are made of. The show went out live, and there was an excitement around the building that I have never known before, or since. People remember it as belonging to an exclusive club. All along the line *Coronation Street* had been *ours*. We gave it to the world.

On and off the Street

Actor William Roache, familiar to everyone as intellectual Ken Barlow, is the only surviving cast member from episode one of *Coronation Street* . . .

William Roache

Seven p.m., Friday night, 9 December 1960 – the first transmission of *Coronation Street* – is burned into my memory with a mixture of fear and excitement. Imagine your most terrifying moment amplified a thousand times, and you might come somewhere near to the experience of live television. It certainly helped to concentrate the mind – we used to learn our lines so well that we could say them in a blackout, and on occasions we had to.

Fearful though it was, there were two occasions when I was almost reduced to giggles, or 'corpsing' as we say in the trade. Both were connected with Ken's father Frank, who was played by the late Frank Pemberton. Ken the university student had no rapport with his postman father, and in one episode Frank, criticizing him for studying a useless subject like history, said: 'I don't know anything about history except King Harold riding about on his horse with his hawk in his hand.' When it came to transmission he said: 'I don't know anything about history except King Harold riding about on his hawk with his horse in his hand.' . . . We somehow managed to keep going. Frank sometimes had trouble with certain words and would write them down in strategic positions around the set.

In the same episode we were sitting down having breakfast, and Frank had written the word on his boiled egg. Now it is a well-known fact that on transmission, with the adrenalin flowing, everything speeds up. And with awful inevitability we saw him smash his egg before he reached the required word, but he managed to continue.

In those early days the Street was a vastly different animal. The pace was much slower, with fewer and longer scenes delving into greater depths of character and situation, and there was far less comedy. There was a greater intensity from all quarters, and more rehearsal time. The change over the years has been gradual, imperceptible, and I think necessary. It reflects society and shows that *Coronation Street* is a living organism. Everything today is quicker, more superficial, and with more comedy. If the Street had not changed in this way, it would not have retained its great following.

However, there are certain values and principles which it has wisely maintained, and these are the key to its huge success. *Coronation Street* shows that community spirit is alive and well, and that people are basically good. Vandalism does not take place where people care what their neighbours think; when the chips are down everyone helps, and you can always borrow a cup of sugar. Grandma and grand-child can sit down and watch the programme together in the sure knowledge that they will be entertained and not offended.

Sir John Betjeman described the Street as Dickensian – an excellent description as it is mainly about characters, and the stories emanate from them, rather than vice versa. This is the twenty-fifth year of *Coronation Street*, and as the only surviving member of the original cast it was perhaps natural that I should be asked what has changed. When change takes place gradually around you, it is rather like ageing. It passes unnoticed until something suddenly makes you stop and look around. I suppose the two major differences are that I am twenty-five years older and two and a half stone heavier. When episode one was shown recently for an anniversary, I arrived for rehearsal the following morning and the director said: 'I'm glad to see you got over your anorexia . . .'

Ken is a one-man Greek tragedy. He has lost his mother, father, brother and not one but two wives. He is the intellectual in the Street, and a responsible sort of chap, so naturally a little heavy. He has gone from university student to newspaper editor via teaching, personnel officer, taxi driver and community development officer – and, of course, three wives and assorted girlfriends. This combination of intelligence and experience has given him a wisdom which makes him a good shoulder to cry on.

The fame, notoriety and exposure of working in the Street is curious. Having been in the top-rated TV show twice a week for twenty-five years, plus enormous coverage in the press, even those who positively dislike the show will have inadvertently seen me at some time or another. It can have its advantages, and quite a few perks. But it was all put into perspective one day when a *Coronation Street* personality was requested to do a personal appearance at some event for quite a good fee. A few hours later the agent concerned rang to say that the personality was no longer needed – they had booked the Brooke Bond chimpanzees instead. It is none the less a test of character to come to terms with the constant recognition, and some pass better than others. A quiet cup of tea at an M1 service station can turn out to be as busy as the shop opening you have just done. Generally people are pleasant and polite, and it is a real joy to see the look of pleasure in the eyes of those who recognize you, particularly the old and the young.

Another strange phenomenon created by a long-running serial is the confusion with reality. This was much stronger in the early days, with people sending wreaths to funerals and presents for birthdays. I remember a woman asking me if I ever minded having a camera in my home, filming everything I did. I took this as a compliment to the reality of the show, something we all took great pains to preserve.

The illusion is much harder to maintain now, with so much being shown behind the scenes on television, and the revelations of the private lives of actors in the daily and Sunday papers. However, there are still many who treat us as 'family', and live vicariously through us. Although we are an entertainment there is a necessary sense of duty and responsibility. I have come to regard Ken as a nickname, and respond readily to: 'Hello Ken, how's the beer in the Rovers?' The identity crisis rests with the viewers – I have had twenty-five years to adjust to the constant recognition.

The adjustment has had definite phases. The first, of realizing that you are known, recognized or famous is heady stuff. You feel great, it is a thing that all actors long for somewhere inside. The 'look at me' syndrome – the child in us crying for love and attention – is a major motivation in becoming an actor, and reveals a state of emotional immaturity. Even so, it is a good feeling – cheques are cashed, night-clubs open their doors, and seats become available in restaurants, as well as the ever-increasing requests for personal appearances.

The second phase is not so pleasant. There is a

feeling of no escape, you cannot run away, and the Sunday papers become menacing. The realization that instant recognition is a two-edged sword dawns with the first minor misdemeanor, or attempt to do anything *incognito*. I arrived at a small village in the Orkneys, and within four minutes everyone knew I was there. It would be hopeless taking up housebreaking as a job.

The third phase, when it all settles, is the realization that you are no better, or worse, than anyone else. You just happen to be known to 90 per cent of the population. It has its good and bad sides, but overall I enjoy it. I play golf and I am invited to take part in some wonderful Pro-Am tournaments alongside top professionals – and I know I am not asked for my playing ability. For the last two years I have been in the winning team at the Benson & Hedges Tournament – with Sandy Lyle last year and Bernhard Langer the year before – and all due to *Coronation Street*.

People often ask me about typecasting and the restrictions it imposes. If typecasting alone were the restriction, then Arthur Lowe would not have progressed so brilliantly from character to character in so many serials and series. The limitation is in the ability, not the casting. Of course certain doors are closed, but just as many are open. I have a production company which I run with my wife Sara, and we find that audiences do turn out to see an entertaining play with a television name in it – but on the night they expect you to produce the goods. As I walk on stage in *Blythe Spirit*, for instance, there is either a round of applause or murmurings of 'that's Ken . . .' After that I have to be convincing, otherwise word soon gets round and bookings are not so good.

The source of all this is *Coronation Street*. I am as pleased to be in it now as I was at the beginning, still feeling that I have a contribution to make and things to learn from it. To be able to say that I have been in the Street for twenty-five years pleases me. And I look forward with enthusiasm to the next twenty-five.

A Coronation Street Who's Who

Some of the main characters of the past twenty-five years.

Mike Baldwin
JOHNNY BRIGGS

Born: 16.2.1942
Education: Secondary Modern, Bermondsey.
Address: The Penthouse Flat, St Mary's Place.

Romeo Mike works hard to maintain his image as the Street's most eligible man. He likes the soft lights and aftershave approach, but most girls get the message a mile away. With his second-hand Jag, seduction sofa and well-stocked drinks cupboard, Mike has 'arrived'. But beneath that smooth appearance is there a lonely heart looking for a soul-mate? On just a few occasions Mike has surprised even himself by falling headlong into love.

He was born in a Bermondsey basement flat, and left school at fifteen to work as a tea boy in a local radio factory. Two years later, with the knowledge he had picked up, he set up a TV and radio repair shop in the family's front bedroom.

Mike discovered that he was a natural businessman and, after several successful ventures, moved into the rag trade. He launched an East End denim factory and, as it prospered, decided to open a branch in the north. 'Baldwin's Casuals', specializing in denim and sports clothes, opened in the Warehouse in Coronation Street.

Mike has a reputation for being a tough, but straight-talking boss. In 1977, threatened with a strike when he intended to transfer work to his London factory, he put his cards on the table, and his staff agreed to work harder to safeguard their jobs.

Mike has a roving eye for the ladies, and the sight of an attractive figure soon has him smoothing back his hair. After moving to Weatherfield he wasted no time persuading Bet Lynch to move in with him. When he tried to get her out by telling Bet that his wife was arriving, the 'wife' turned out to be another mistress.

Mike has a robust constitution, too. After a timber lorry had ploughed into the Rovers in 1979, he was pulled from the debris with a crushed leg and fractured ribs. When a dispute flared at the factory Mike, still injured, discharged himself from hospital to deal with it.

David Barlow
ALAN ROTHWELL

Born: 4.7.1942
Died: 10.4.1970
Education: Bessie Street Junior and Senior Schools.

After playing part-time soccer with local county sides, Ken's sporty brother David turned professional and joined a Southern League club. While Ken worried and kept things to himself, David was the easy-going extrovert. He married Stan and Hilda's daughter Irma, and they ran the Corner Shop together for two years until emigrating to Australia in 1968. David and his two-year-old son Darren were killed in a car crash there in 1970.

Deirdre Barlow
ANNE KIRKBRIDE

Born: 8.7.1955
Education: Bessie Street Schools, Weatherfield Commercial College.
Address: 1 Coronation Street.

Behind those picture-frame glasses beats the heart of a passionate woman. In her Corner Shop overall, Deirdre is the hard-working wife and mum. Off duty she needs to feel feminine – when lukewarm Ken slid into lethargy and failed to pay her enough attention, Deirdre lived dangerously and dived into a determined affair with romeo Mike Baldwin. She had always been attracted to undependable men, and her marriage to steady Ken hit rocky patches. Deirdre was engaged to roving Billy Walker in 1975 but, to Annie Walker's visible relief, had second thoughts and called off the wedding a month before the date.

Almost immediately she plunged into a love-hate relationship with reckless Ray Langton. Ray had a knack of making most people see red. With Deirdre it turned to romance, and they were married in the summer of 1975. Two years later their daughter Tracey was born, but Deirdre's world crashed when she discovered that Ray had been having an affair with a waitress. Knowing that she could never trust him again, they parted in November 1978, and Ray moved to Holland.

Deirdre's life revolved completely around Tracey. She was distraught when she thought her toddler had been killed by a timber wagon which crashed into the Rovers, but Tracey was found safe in a local park. Friendship with Ken blossomed after a date at a local disco, and they married in 1981. Despite her affair with Mike, and Ken's fling with Sally Waterman, life for the moment seems to be running smoothly.

Frank Barlow
FRANK PEMBERTON

Born: 19.10.1913
Died: 21.4.1975
Education: Weatherfield Council School.

Pipe-smoking Frank appeared in the first episode of the Street, voicing his disapproval of his son Ken's middle-class girlfriend. Frank was staunchly working class and believed it could only lead to trouble. His quiet manner belied the fact that he had won a Military Medal during heavy action in Iraq. Like many of his generation he was strongly against hire purchase, and proudly believed in 'paying his way'. Frank retired as a GPO supervisor to open one of Weatherfield's first DIY shops, in Victoria Street. His wife Ida was killed beneath the wheels of a bus in 1961. Frank retired to a detached house in Wilmslow after a £5,000 Premium Bond win, where he died in 1975.

Ida Barlow
NOEL DYSON

Born: 16.12.1916
Died: 11.9.1961
Education: Weatherfield Elementary School.

  Hard-working Ida left school at fourteen to work in Ernshaw's Mill. She married Frank in 1938 and worked as a kitchen help in the Imperial Hotel until her death. Ida allowed independent David to go his own way, but worried about Ken's left-wing views and his girlfriends. Ida lived for her family and, just before her death, had persuaded her ageing mother, Nancy Leathers, to live with them.

Irma Barlow
SANDRA GOUGH

Born: 28.9.1946
Education: Bessie Street Schools.

  Fun-loving Irma, Stan and Hilda Ogden's daughter, was a natural mimic, and won second prize in a talent contest for her impersonations. She left school at fifteen, acquired a beehive hairstyle, and took a job in the raincoat factory. She married David Barlow in 1966 and they left for Australia in 1968. When her husband and son were killed in 1970, Irma flew home with Hilda, who had arrived to comfort her. She left the Street in 1972 for Llandudno, and is now building a new life in Canada.

Ken Barlow
WILLIAM ROACHE

Born: 9.10.1939
Education: University. Second Class Honours in History and English.
Address: 1 Coronation Street.

Solid Ken is one of the Street's most durable characters. He has lost his family and two wives, yet somehow soldiers on. Despite his liberal views, he is a stick-in-the-mud, preferring to stay in Weatherfield to using his degree to build a career. Deirdre, his third wife, finds him dependable, but is occasionally bored by his lack of adventure.

Ken is the son of Post Office supervisor Frank Barlow who retired and went into the DIY business. He was bright at school and gained a university place without difficulty.

In his younger days he was a rebel, and in 1967 was jailed for taking part in an anti-Vietnam War demonstration which had been banned by the police. He wrote a hard-hitting article about the working classes for a left-wing review, which caused concern in the Street and a fight with Len Fairclough.

Ken's mother Ida died under the wheels of a bus in 1961. His father Frank and brother David are both deceased. He has been a personnel officer, teacher, failed novelist, junior warehouse executive, taxi driver, and is now a newspaper editor. In 1971 his first wife, Valerie, was electrocuted by a faulty hair-dryer plug, and his second, Janet, committed suicide with barbiturates some time after their divorce. The children live with Val's mother in Glasgow.

Ken has had several affairs during and between his marriages. A holiday at the Lakes with Deirdre Langton brought threats from her estranged husband Ray to cite him as co-respondent. Fearing the publicity would cost him his job, he tried to back out before he realized that he was in love and decided to stand by her. He is now married to Deirdre and her daughter Tracey lives with them.

He has a life-long weakness for intelligent, independent women, and in 1985 almost plunged into a passionate affair with reporter Sally Waterman.

Valerie Barlow
ANNE REID

Born: 26.11.1942
Died: 27.1.1971
Education: Bessie Street Primary, Weatherfield Secondary Modern, and the Weatherfield School of Hairdressing.

Val met Ken Barlow for the first time when she left her parents in Glasgow to live with her uncle, Albert Tatlock, in Coronation Street. They married in 1962, and had twins three years later. Hairdresser Val felt inferior to Ken's intellectual friends, to the point of enrolling at nightschool to 'improve' herself. She believed in him completely, and backed him when he wanted to throw in his job and become a writer. Secretly she worried about the money, but did not want to sound mundane. The twins – 5lb 3oz Susan and Peter who weighed in at 4lb 11oz – were born in Weatherfield General when Len Fairclough rushed Val to hospital in his van. She was electrocuted by a faulty hair-dryer plug when the children were six years old.

Suzie Birchall
CHERYL MURRAY

Born: 3.5.1958
Education: Weatherfield Girls Secondary Modern.
Address: Formerly 11 Coronation Street. Now lives in London.

Cheeky blonde Suzie arrived in the Street looking for work in 1976, and her figure soon caught Mike Baldwin's eye. He offered her a job displaying denims in his shop, 'The Western Front'. Suzie lodged with Elsie Howard (Tanner) and Gail Potter at No. 11. She came from a broken home, and her overbearing father tried to force her to return to look after him when his wife had gone, but her boyfriend Steve Fisher stood by her.

Flighty, frivolous Suzie was a natural survivor with an appetite for excitement. She left the Street to seek her fortune in London, and returned in a high-powered car with a middle-aged romeo at the wheel, boasting about her high-life in the West End. A phone call from her London landlady, answered by Elsie, revealed that she was in debt, and the trip was a failure.

When Suzie picked up a punk rocker, Mike Baldwin told her she would have to choose between them. Suzie chose the punk and Mike wasted no time firing her from the factory. She left the Street for London again at Christmas 1979, returning four years later to confess that she was married. Her husband Terry followed her and beat her up. Bruised Suzie was last seen accepting a lift from a travelling salesman heading in the direction of Blackburn.

Sheila Birtles
EILEEN MYERS

Born: 23.4.1940
Education: Rawtenstall Secondary Modern.
Address: Now living in Sheffield.

Scatty Sheila and her friend Doreen Lostock, curled up in their bed-sit swopping girl-talk, were one of the funniest double-acts in the Street. She worked in the raincoat factory and, with her headscarf protecting her hair-do, lost no time in setting her sights on bashful Jerry Booth. He took her for a day in the country – on the back of his tandem. Jerry, and her parents, objected strongly when Sheila took a liking to fast-talking Liverpudlian Jed Stone, and ran a market stall with him. After an abortive suicide bid she married shop manager Neil Crossley in 1967, by whom she had had an illegitimate child. They left the Street for Scarborough, and are now living in Sheffield.

Emily Bishop
EILEEN DERBYSHIRE

Born: 18.10.1929
Education: Henley Road High School for Girls.
Address: 3 Coronation Street.

Straightlaced Emily is quiet and anxious not to offend, but her lofty standards have led to an unhappy love-life. She was engaged to marry Leonard Swindley, but called it off on her wedding day. Her search for romance took her to a marriage bureau, but the introductions were unsuccessful. She fell for a macho Hungarian building worker who was afraid of settling down. And once, as leader of a local playgroup, she was attracted to Weatherfield's vicar, but found his convictions too weak. Her second husband Arnold broke her heart when he was unmasked as a bigamist. Emily is not without admirers – Percy Sugden secretly loves her – but as an ex-draper she knows that only quality really counts.

Emily's father, Edward Nugent, a member of the Corps of Commissionaires, and her mother Agnes are both dead. Her only surviving relative is her sister Norah, who is married to former Coventry city councillor Stuart Seddon.

Emily works at Baldwin's Casuals in a similar clerical job to her first husband Ernest, who was killed in a wage raid on the factory. She married Ernest, who had similar interests in religion and photography, on Easter Monday 1972, and they became supporters of every local good cause. When their marriage went through a difficult patch the Bishops temporarily fostered two black children.

Churchgoer Emily worked hard to keep their home together. When their photographic business failed, she sold her engagement ring and became a hospital orderly – but drew the line at Ernest playing the piano to accompany strippers at a local night-club.

Emily passed her driving test in 1965, but has since been too nervous to sit behind the wheel. In 1985 she was the landlady of Curly Watts and Kevin Webster.

Ernest Bishop
STEPHEN HANCOCK

Born: 21.8.1930
Died: 11.1.1978
Education: Scholarship from Bessie Street Elementary School to Weatherfield Grammar. Qualified at Granston Tech as a Fellow of the Institute of British Photography.

Ernest followed in the footsteps of his photographer father George, who died in 1956. His mother Caroline passed away at the age of seventy in 1969. At her funeral he met shy Emily Nugent and they became engaged two years later.

Courtship was clouded by a photographic assignment to Spain when Ernest, Congregational lay preacher, was jailed for offending public morality. Models had been hired to pose with a business delegation and, in the course of a group photograph, the atmosphere – to Ernest's consternation – became sexually heated.

He was a competent pianist, and acted as Rita Fairclough's accompanist when she sang at night-clubs. He became Mike Baldwin's pay clerk and right-hand man when the factory opened in 1976 until his tragic death three years later. Two raiders, armed with a sawn-off shotgun, burst into his office demanding cash. Ernest tried to reason with them, but they panicked when Mike Baldwin walked in. Ernest was shot, and died on the operating table at Weatherfield Infirmary.

Jerry Booth
GRAHAM HABERFIELD

Born: 2.8.1941
Died: 10.11.1975
Education: Bessie Street Schools. Evening classes – two O-levels.

Plumber Jerry was born in Viaduct Street, and served his apprenticeship with Joe White, of Bessie Street. He was a keen cyclist, and rode with Weatherfield Wheelers, but was tongue-tied with girls. Myra Dickinson understood him, and they married in 1963. Their daughter died at birth, and the marriage slowly fell apart until four years later, they were divorced. Jerry proposed to Sheila Birtles, but she eloped with Neil Crossley. Another romance, with librarian Sally Frost, broke up. Jerry left the Street quietly after his speech as best man at Dennis Tanner's wedding in 1968. He returned briefly a few years later, but died of pneumonia in 1975.

Myra Booth

SUSAN JAMIESON

Moody Myra Dickinson's marriage to Jerry Booth ran into money trouble when they failed to keep up their mortgage payments. Myra was hopeless with cash – whenever Jerry handed her the housekeeping, it disappeared within days. Before the divorce was absolute, she pleaded for a reconciliation. When that failed Myra tried to force Rovers landlord Jack Walker to testify that she and Jerry had been seeing each other. Living without Jerry proved almost as hard as living with him. When they separated she had to send her father to borrow money from him, and kind-hearted Jerry obliged. Myra's present whereabouts are unknown.

Minnie Caldwell

MARGOT BRYANT

Born: 30.9.1900
Education: Hardcastle's Factory School.
Address: Now living in Whalley Bridge.

Mild, mouse-like Minnie was never allowed a word in edgeways by her bossy friend Ena Sharples. There were times when she preferred the company of her cat Bobbie – at least he could not answer back. Mill-girl Minnie's husband, Armistead, died in 1935. Her working life was spent in Hardcastle's and Pemberton's mills, except for a spell on wartime munitions at Greenhalgh's in Derby Street.

When her mother died in 1962, Minnie moved into No. 5 and took in Jed Stone as a lodger. She was a secret gambler with a knack for picking winners. At one time the habit was so strong that friends begged the local bookie to restrict her betting. Minnie had a widow's eye for Street romances, occasionally stepping in unasked as matchmaker. She agreed to marry Albert Tatlock to improve her pension, but called it off when she found that she would be worse off financially. Minnie left the Street in April 1976 to live in Whalley Bridge, where she still keeps house for an old schoolfriend, Handel Gartside.

Ivan Cheveski
ERNST WALDER
Linda Cheveski
ANNE CUNNINGHAM

Handsome Czech engineer Ivan married Elsie Tanner's daughter Linda. She fell downstairs when she was pregnant, but their son Paul was safely born at a healthy 7lb 2oz in 1961. The marriage was an on-off affair, punctuated with rows and reconciliations. They emigrated to Montreal when Paul was six months old, hoping to start afresh. Linda was unfaithful in Canada, and Ivan returned home alone to take a job in Birmingham. Linda followed and wrote to her Canadian lover, ending the affair. She returned briefly to the Street in 1984, and is now back in Birmingham with Ivan.

Harry Clayton
JOHNNY LEEZE
Connie Clayton
SUSAN BROWN

Andrea Clayton
CAROLE O'NEILL
Sue Clayton
JANE HAZLEGROVE

Milkman Harry and his family moved into the Street in 1985 after buying the Webster's house. Brainy Andrea, aged eighteen, has her sights on furthering her education, while headstrong Sue, with poor CSE results and no ambition, always hated school. Happy-go-lucky Harry plays trombone with Gregg Gordon and the Bluetones, while dressmaker Connie takes in tailoring alterations. But, as Vera Duckworth found to her cost, asking a neighbour does not always work out cheaper.

Les Clegg
JOHN SHARP

Born: 7.4.1918
Education: Elementary and Senior Council Schools.

Les, an ex-corporal in the Lancashire Fusiliers, was a warehouse clerk who dreamed of running his own business. He bought the Corner Shop, but sought relief from the responsibility in heavy drinking. He was friendly with Rovers landlord Jack Walker, and went bowling with him. After hospital treatment for alcoholism, Les took a job in a Solihull furniture warehouse, and still lives in the midlands.

Gordon Clegg
BILL KENWRIGHT

Born: 20.5.1950
Education: Clackers Lane Elementary School. Weatherfield Grammar.
Address: Now living in London.

Gordon, an only child, fell for tearaway Lucille Hewitt soon after moving to the Street. They eloped to Gretna Green, but had second thoughts. Ambitious Gordon later bought her an engagement ring with a £5 examination prize, but grew away from working class Coronation Street when he passed his accountancy finals. Lucille kept the ring, and Gordon left in 1969 when his firm transferred him to London. He returned briefly to oversee the sale of the shop, and returned to the City, where he is now happily married.

Jack Duckworth
BILL TARMEY

Born: 7.11.1934
Education: Rochdale Road Secondary Modern.
Address: 9 Coronation Street.

Gravel-voiced Jack is always looking for the main chance – but his efforts to make fast money or have a romantic fling on his window-cleaning round end in disaster. Jack loves life in the fast lane, but never seems to get off the hard shoulder. On the rare occasions he dresses up, with his *Saturday Night Fever* shirt slashed to the waist and his tarnished medallion, he is the oldest swinger in the Street. Vera may not be impressed, but Jack thinks he's terrific.

Work is one of his biggest worries – not finding it, but avoiding it. He lives by the law of least effort. Chopping the top off Percy Sugden's Christmas tree, instead of walking to the shop and buying one, is the classic Duckworth response to life's little problems. Jack first appeared in the Street at Gail and Brian's wedding and has been around ever since. He has tried taxi-driving, running a market stall, and still privately believes that Newton and Ridley were crazy not to make him manager of the Rovers.

Maggie Clegg
IRENE SUTCLIFFE

Born: 12.6.1924
Education: Clackers Lane Elementary and Senior Schools.
Address: Now living in Zaire.

Cheerful Maggie ran the Corner Shop with her alcoholic husband Les, and accountant son Gordon. She met Les in wartime, while working at the Food Office, and they married in 1946. When Gordon was born Maggie became a school dinner lady until Les invested in the shop in 1968. She was interested in herbalism and stocked natural remedies. Anxious Maggie watched Les's drink problem worsen, and become more violent, until he was admitted to a mental hospital. When they divorced, Maggie accepted a £600 partnership in the business from widow Irma Barlow. Gordon's real mother was Maggie's sister Betty Turpin, but understanding Maggie brought him up because he was illegitimate. She doted on him and disapproved of his engagement to Lucille Hewitt, fearing it would hold back his career. Maggie married reformed alcoholic Ron Cooke in 1974, and left the Street to live in Zaire.

40

Vera Duckworth
ELIZABETH DAWN

Born: 3.9.1936
Education: Moss Side Secondary Modern.
Address: 9 Coronation Street.

Vera is a bubble-haired blonde with a bawdy sense of humour, and a voice like a fog horn on the Ship Canal. She calls everyone 'kid', and only takes out her chewing gum when she dresses up. Like Jack, it is Weatherfield Market's answer to the drop-dead look – plus half a pound of mascara, and a bulk supply of lipstick for the biggest mouth in the Street. She spoils 'our Terry', while Jack gets little sympathy at all. Vera was first seen when Fred Gee was given permission to entertain a lady friend at the Rovers. When Annie Walker saw her she was so horrified that she played gooseberry to scotch Fred's chances. Vera and Jack were separated at the time, but patched up their marriage.

She is keen on money, and stirred shop steward Ivy Tilsley into battles with the management as soon as she started at the factory. When the firm threatened short-time working, Vera instantly got herself a job at the supermarket. She is a bit thick, but as crafty as a barrowload of monkeys – and to keep ahead of Jack she has to be.

Terry Duckworth
NIGEL PIVARO

Born: 4.6.1964
Education: Bessie Street Secondary Modern.
Address: 9 Coronation Street.

Sharp-talking Terry was on the dole after leaving school, until he joined the Parachute Regiment as a trainee in 1982. He failed the course and returned home to work in Weatherfield abattoir. Terry has little respect for his dad, and sides with Vera to browbeat him into finding work. But, like Jack, he has an unshakable belief in his power over women. Cocky Terry inherits his mum's craftiness, and usually gets his own way when talking pals into his devious plans.

Len Fairclough
PETER ADAMSON

Born: 5.11.1924
Died: 7.12.1983

Rough and ready Len boozed and brawled his way through the Street's early episodes to become a respected businessman and local councillor. He was a self-made man with a measure of financial success, but found long-term relationships hard to handle. Even when happily married to Rita he was having a secret affair.

Hot-tempered Len was born on bonfire night at the height of a Liverpool firework display. As a youngster he was known as Tearaway Len by his pals who played in the city's tough Scotland Road area. His parents, Ned and Grace, were both killed in a dockland air-raid in 1941.

Len left school at fourteen to become an apprentice bricklayer with Hunt Bros. When the war intervened he served with the Royal Navy on the Russian convoys. After demob he moved to Weatherfield when the firm opened a branch in Clarence Street. Len became self-employed in 1962 and bought a yard at 15 Mawdesley Street.

Partnerships with Jerry Booth and Ray Langton followed.

Len married his first wife, Nellie Briggs, in 1949, but she left him in 1962, taking their twelve-year-old son Stanley with her. A year later they were divorced, and Nellie died of cancer in 1964. Stanley tried to live with his abrasive dad, but hated working-class life in the Street.

Len proposed to Elsie Tanner on several occasions, but each time she turned him down. He was once engaged to Janet Reid, Ken Barlow's second wife, but the romance ended when she admitted she had no real feelings for him. In 1975 Len had a tempestuous affair with Bet Lynch, but they split up when he refused to live with her. Then he fell for red-haired night-club singer Rita Littlewood, and persuaded her to cancel a booking in Teneriffe and become Mrs Fairclough. They married on 20 April 1977, but not without an anxious moment – Len was late when his taxi had a flat tyre.

In December 1983 he was killed in a motorway accident. To add to her heartbreak Rita discovered that, at the time of the crash, Len had been seeing another woman, and was returning from a date with her.

Rita Fairclough

BARBARA KNOX

Born: 25.2.1932
Education: Fallowfield Elementary School.
Address: 7 Coronation Street.

Red-haired Rita Littlewood always loved the limelight, and took her first showbiz steps at the age of four, when she enjoyed singing and dancing at family parties. Her father Harold walked out on the family when she was six, and her mother Amy died of cancer in 1956. Rita left school at fourteen to work in a grocery store, but still yearned for the bright lights. At eighteen she plucked up courage to gatecrash an audition, and spent the next few years touring the north and midlands in panto and third-rate revues.

She first appeared in Weatherfield as a dancer at the Orinoco Club, when Dennis Tanner was assistant manager. In 1968 she met construction worker Harry Bates, who was separated, and embarked on an unhappy affair. Harry's children, Terry and Gail, needed a mother, and soft-hearted Rita moved in to become 'Mrs Bates'.

She met Councillor Len Fairclough at a school parents' meeting in 1972, and asked him to help her get a council house. When Harry Bates discovered that she was having a furtive affair with Len, he beat her up and threw her out of the house. Len was given a warning by the Mayor, and broke off the friendship.

Rita, abandoned again, reverted to her old name Littlewood. A few months later she ran into Len in a local club, and the affair rekindled. Rita broke off her engagement when she suspected him of being unfaithful, but they patched up their differences and married in 1977. Now widowed, she still works in the Kabin, the shop they built up together. Rita found happiness with Len, but would have liked children – she cared for Terry and Gail Bates, enjoyed fostering Sharon Gaskell, and even mothers Mavis Riley through her troubles.

Len's memory is a hurdle she finds hard to overcome. Rugged Detective Inspector Tony Cunliffe asked her to spend Christmas with him, but realized that Rita was not ready for an affair.

Fred Gee
FRED FEAST

Born: 7.10.1934
Education: Bessie Street Schools.
Address: Whereabouts unknown.

Frustrated Fred was brash and chatty with the men of the Street. But behind the Rovers bar he was surrounded by women – and they could see through all his schemes. Annie's sharp tongue made him furtive, he bridled at Bet's put-downs and gave way to Betty's bossiness.

Fred left school at fifteen, and worked as a labourer and a storeman at Foster's. In 1976, a year after his wife Edna died in the warehouse fire, Fred left his home in Inkerman Street and moved into the Rovers as resident bar/cellarman.

Lusty passions lay beneath that tubby exterior, but the roly-poly romeo was destined to join life's great unfulfilled. His blood pressure rose for newly-separated Vera Duckworth, but Annie Walker played gooseberry and Vera went back to her husband. He was promised a pub of his own by the brewery, provided he married again. Fred's pulse quickened – but a succession of women turned him down.

He also fell for Rita Littlewood before she married, and wooed her with a single red rose. It made little difference – she gave him the cold shoulder too – but he still carried a torch for her. Fred's second marriage, to Eunice Nuttall in 1981, was part of his ploy to get the licence of the Crown and Kettle. But, typical of Fred, it nosedived, and Eunice upset Betty by acting as

though she owned the Rovers. They moved to the Community Centre until Fred was sacked for insulting people. When the Gees were offered a chance to manage the Park View Hotel, Weatherfield, Eunice accepted, but Fred stayed in the Street and the marriage broke up.

He left the Street a few months after Billy Walker took over the Rovers in August 1984 and fired him. Furious Fred's farewell was to punch him on the nose.

Dot Greenhalgh
JOAN FRANCIS

Elsie Tanner's friend Dot worked with her at Miami Modes, and provided a shoulder to cry on. She was not as loyal as she first appeared, letting Elsie take the blame and appear in court on a charge of stealing coats from the shop. Dot, a stylish dresser, has since disappeared with her husband Walter, and her whereabouts are unknown.

Bill Gregory
JACK WATSON

Rugged Bill was a wartime friend of Len who fell for Elsie in a big way, but omitted to tell her he was married. He was sick of his wife Phyllis, but did not have the strength of character to end it. Bill wanted Elsie to commit herself before he left home for good. But Elsie – despite her weakness for uniforms – refused to be the 'other woman'. Eventually Chief Petty Officer Gregory went back to his wife. Years later, retired from the sea, he called on Elsie and asked her to live with him in Portugal. They are still there, running Gregory's Bar together, in the Algarve.

Christine Hardman
CHRISTINE HARGREAVES

Cheery Christine had an unhappy side. In the early episodes of the Street she suffered a nervous breakdown, and had to be talked down from the factory roof by Ken Barlow. On impulse she married Colin Appleby, who was later killed in a car crash. Still searching for security, Christine became engaged to Ken's widower father Frank. They called it off because of their age difference, and she left the Street in 1963.

Concepta Hewitt
DOREEN KEOGH

Harry Hewitt
IVAN BEAVIS

Bus inspector Harry, a shy widower with a sense of humour, married the Rovers Irish barmaid Concepta in 1961. A year later they had a son, Christopher, who was kidnapped but returned safely on their first wedding anniversary. The Hewitts left to live in Ireland. When they returned for a Street wedding in 1967, Harry was killed when a jack collapsed and Len Fairclough's van fell on him. Concepta remarried Sean, an Irishman with a roving eye, and lives in Castle Blaney, Eire, with Harry's daughter Lucille.

Lucille Hewitt
JENNIFER MOSS

Born: 4.5.1949
Education: Bessie Street School. Weatherfield Grammar, four O-levels.
Address: Now living in Castle Blaney, Eire.

Wayward Lucille was the Street's first teenage rebel. She horrified her headmistress by dying her urchin hair blonde, and having her arm tattooed. When Harry and Concepta moved to Ireland, she refused to follow and lodged at the Rovers, where Annie Walker's strict rules irritated her. Impulsive Lucille eloped, became a vegetarian, followed pop star Brett Falcon to London, and joined a hippy commune. Still unpredictable, she has finally settled down in Ireland.

Alan Howard
ALAN BROWNING

Born: 23.4.1924
Education: Newcastle Grammar School.

Dapper Alan Howard liked to do things in style, even if he could not afford it. Elsie Tanner first noticed him when he opened his hairdressing salon with a champagne reception. They married in 1970, but businessman Alan had problems handling money, and soon found himself on the verge of bankruptcy. They drifted apart and were divorced in 1978. Alan remarried Elaine Dennet, and now lives back in his hometown, Newcastle.

Blanche Hunt
MAGGIE JONES

Deirdre Barlow's footloose and fancy-free mum had several men-friends in the Street, but settled for wealthy bookie Dave Smith. She left Weatherfield in 1976 to live with him in Kennilworth, where they run a country club.

Ray Langton
NEVILLE BUSWELL

Born: 18.2.1947
Education: Bessie Street Schools. Approved school.
Address: Now living in Holland.

Raymond Anthony Langton – the Street's Mr Nasty – was born in Gas Street, behind Weatherfield Police Station a place he came to know well in his formative years. As a youngster he was placed in the care of the local authority when his mother Mary died. He became a juvenile delinquent and was sent to an approved school, where he learned the basics of plumbing and joinery. Ray left Bessie Street School at fifteen and served a two-year apprenticeship as a plumber and joiner with Harold Roberts, of Gas Street.

In 1965 he joined Len Fairclough, but was sacked for stealing. Later he spent two years in jail for breaking and entering, but was taken back by Len in 1968. Two years later they decided to become partners.

With the exception of a brief fling with textile tycoon's daugter Sue Silcock, he had no steady girlfriends until he was twenty-eight. After a stormy courtship, he married Len's secretary Deirdre Hunt in 1975. Two years later their daughter Tracey was born, and they moved into No. 5 Coronation Street. Within months he was dating waitress Janice Stubbs, until Deirdre confronted him. Penitent Ray begged her to leave the Street and make a fresh start, but she turned him down. The marriage broke up and Ray left to work in Holland in 1978.

Florrie Lindley
BETTY ALBERGE

Friendly Florrie arrived in the Street in episode one to take over the Corner Shop. She was a worrier, but unafraid of crossing swords with busybody Ena Sharples. Her engineer husband Norman was away for six years, and they led separate lives. Florrie suffered a nervous breakdown after an unhappy affair with Frank Barlow, and mounting money problems. Long-lost Norman returned, not to comfort her, but to date Elsie Tanner. The Lindleys decided to make a fresh start and emigrated to Canada in 1965.

Martha Longhurst
LYNNE CAROL

Born: 2.9.1899
Died: 13.5.1964
Education: Hardcastle's Factory School.

Bespectacled Martha lived in Mawdesley Street and, with Ena Sharples and Minnie Caldwell, made up the formidable Mafia of the Rovers Snug. She was almost as nosey as Ena, and never missed any Street gossip. Martha, a cleaner at the pub, nursed high hopes of an affair with old schoolfriend, Ted Ashley. It blossomed as far as a trip to London together, but Martha died unexpectedly from a heart attack in her second home, the Snug.

Bet Lynch

JULIE GOODYEAR

Born: 4.5.1940
Education: Bessie Street Schools.
Address: Rovers Return, Coronation Street.

Blonde, busty Bet is a tough nut with a marshmallow centre. She was born in Clegg Street, Weatherfield, where her father Patrick walked out on the family when she was six months old, and was never seen again. As a teenager Bet was a hell-raiser. At sixteen she became pregnant and had an illegitimate son, Martin. He was adopted at six weeks old when Bet's mother Mary threatened to throw her out of the house.

After the birth she worked as a shop assistant, and later as a machinist at Elliston's raincoat factory, where she had an affair with the foreman. Bet took a job in a launderette, and had various digs until she settled in the Street in 1970. She was taken on at the Rovers by Billy Walker, against the wishes of his mother Annie who found her 'common'. It was an unsettled time – Bet was mugged in 1973 and, the following year, attempted suicide when she heard that her son had been killed in a car crash while serving as a soldier in Northern Ireland.

Brassy Bet has firm ideas about fashion, which lean towards the acrylic, and a large collection of eye-stopping earrings. What they lack in discretion, they make up for in size. For special occasions she wears a pair featuring portraits of Prince Charles and Princess Diana.

Her 'conquests' include county footballer Eddie Duncan, Len Fairclough, and Mike Baldwin. But Bet, a loser in love, is usually left in the lurch. Early in 1985, against strong competition, her years of pint-pulling in the Rovers were rewarded when the brewery appointed her manageress, and she moved into the pub. A lifetime of Bet and beer will be a rare catch for someone.

Hilda Ogden
JEAN ALEXANDER

Born: 24.2.1924
Education: St Joseph's Elementary School.
Address: 13 Coronation Street.

When husband Stan was alive Hilda liked to regard herself, not as the street's Mrs Mopp, but as the wife of a company executive. Behind the curtains of No. 13, however, her efforts to persuade Stan to work industriously on his window-cleaning round usually met with failure.

Hilda has always taken a pride in boosting her income by running several cleaning jobs simultaneously. Her scrawny figure, polishing away in her flowered pinny, has been a familiar early morning sight in the Rovers for years. After Stan's death she took in lodger Henry Wakefield and glowed with pleasure ironing his shirts and cooking dinner.

The Street has kept few secrets from Hilda. Beneath that tightly-bound turban is a highly-tuned sense of hearing. Three rollers poke out inquisitively like radar antennae, constantly scanning for signs of gossip. The more news she tunes into, the faster she polishes. Hilda has a soft-spot for the underdog – after all, she married Stan – and offers help and advice to anyone who might need it. If they don't, she takes umbrage very quickly.

Hilda is one of the Street's most law-abiding citizens. When Stan brewed beer in the bath during the brewery strike, she pulled out the plug in case it was illegal; when he bought cut-price fabric from 'Billy Oilcloth' on the market, she sold it at a loss, fearing it was stolen. Stan, of course, was stunned, but her conscience was clear.

Despite her failure to scale life's social peaks, Hilda will always have one thing no one can take from her – the 'gift' of clairvoyance. Her tea-cup readings may not always be accurate, but it's the way she tells them that's spellbinding.

Stan Ogden
BERNARD YOUENS

Born: 17.5.1919
Died: 21.11.1984
Education: Bessie Street Schools.

Stan was born in Kitchener Street, Weatherfield, and left school at fourteen. In 1941 he went into uniform and joined the Royal Army Service Corps, where he obtained his HGV licence. During the war he married coy, slim Hilda Crabtree, and eventually they set up home in Coronation Street.

In Civvy Street Stan drove lorries for Gaston's until 1964 – the longest he ever stayed in one job. He tried his hand as a chauffeur – which lasted one day – coalman, milkman, and ice-cream seller, before throwing in the towel and signing on the dole for two years. Stan finally settled down to window-cleaning, a calling to which he was ideally suited as everyone could see right through him.

Stan and Hilda had the Street's longest and most successful marriage, even though work was not one of his strong points. But things did not always run smoothly. Stan had one vice – apart from Newton and Ridley's bitter – a mystery woman at 19 Inkerman Street, on his window-cleaning round. Vigilant Hilda poured cold water on the liaison on more than one occasion – until she realized that Stan had given up because he was past it.

Stan and Hilda were usually broke, but believed in the great northern tradition of 'paying your way'. They had cleared up their mortgage by 1965, and bought their daughter Irma a partnership in the Corner Shop. Stan the Superslob, and hard-working Hilda struggling to score social points, were two of a kind. As they stumbled through life's minefield together they made one of the Street's funniest, and most poignant, partnerships. Even in death Hilda would not allow him to be faulted. The funeral, fully paid for, was the Ogden's most lavish and dignified occasion. Sadly, Stan was not alive to share it. There was a glimpse of nobility in Hilda's grief. And on the headstone, which she selected herself, she made sure there was room for two names.

Phyllis Pearce

JILL SUMMERS

Born: 7.2.1921
Address: 4 Gorton Close, Weatherfield.

Bossy, blue-rinsed Phyllis likes a man who 'gets things done'. In the Street that can only mean Percy Sugden, and she visibly melts in his presence. Percy, full of his own importance, refuses to take her on. Perhaps he remembers the days when Phyllis made Chalkie Whiteley's life a misery with her constant carping. She would pop round daily to check that her grandson Craig was being fed properly, and never missed an opportunity to tell him that he was not fit to look after the lad. When Phyllis's home in Ondurman Street was demolished she asked a horrified Chalkie if she could move in with him. He refused, and now Phyllis seems determined to snare poor Percy. Perhaps he isn't as daft as he behaves.

Mavis Riley

THELMA BARLOW

Born: 9.4.1937
Education: Weatherfield Girls School.
Address: The Kabin Flat, 14 Rosamund Street.

Mavis was probably born with a flutter and a sigh. Sometimes described as the 'eternal virgin', she led a sheltered childhood in a strict Methodist household. Her best schoolfriend was Emily Bishop, and later they worked together at the Mark Brittain Warehouse. Her first meeting with the Street residents was at Emily's wedding in 1972, where she met Jerry Booth.

Her parents, George and Margaret, moved to Grange-over-Sands, and timid Mavis hoped that Jerry would propose. When he told her he had been divorced, she fled in shock to Grange. But her heart was still in Weatherfield, and she returned three months later to work as a vet's receptionist. Then, bored with pampered poodles, she quit and took a job at the Corner Shop helping Maggie Clegg. When the business was sold, Rita twisted Len's arm and she was taken on at the Kabin.

Mavis lives alone with her budgie Harriet, waiting for Mr Right to come along. In 1984 two rivals were fighting for her affection, sending her into agonies of palpitating indecision. Finally she ditched old flame Victor Pendlebury, and apprehensively agreed to marry Derek Wilton, who was dominated by his mother. On her wedding day her nerve gave way, and she backed out. Mavis' guilt was eased only by the news that Derek had done the same – then the relief was soon replaced by flushed indignation.

Alf Roberts

BRYAN MOSLEY

Born: 8.10.1926
Address: The Corner Shop, Coronation Street.

Alf is the Street's committee man – Independent member of Weatherfield Council, ex-Post Office Union official, and thoroughly at home with his VAT returns. Twice married, and now widowed, he divides his time between the Corner Shop and Council business.

Alf married his first wife, Phyllis, the year he was demobbed from the Royal Corps of Signals. Two years after her death in 1972 he proposed to Maggie Clegg, who owned the Corner Shop, but she turned him down. On the rebound he met pushy Post Office canteen worker Donna Parker, who let him down by borrowing £500 to start a hairdressing business and disappearing.

Alf, an awkward romeo, courted Renee Bradshaw, who bought the Corner Shop from Maggie, and they married in 1978, just twelve months before he took early retirement as a GPO supervisor. He left the Post Office at fifty-three, with £800 compensation for injuries received when a timber lorry crashed into the Rovers Snug. Renee was tragically killed in a road accident in 1980. Alf, with never a Brylcreemed hair out of place, secretly fancies Rita, but she prefers to regard him as nothing more than a friend. Alf manages to stay cheerful, and rarely refers to his own troubles.

Renee Roberts
MADGE HINDLE

Born: 3.3.1943
Died: 30.7.1980
Education: Weatherfield High School. Six
O-levels.

Renee was brought up in Gas Street, and moved to Lancaster when her father Harold, an insurance clerk, died in 1969. Within three years her widowed mother Daisy had married shifty layabout Joe Hibbert. Renee and her younger brother Terry soon left home.

With her experience as an insurance clerk and as a cashier at a Lancaster supermarket, she developed a good business sense, and bought the Corner Shop with a bank loan in 1976. Terry, who had served in the army, joined her for a while but, disillusioned with civilian life, rejoined the Colours.

Renee was strong-willed and single-minded. She applied for an off-licence for the shop against formidable opposition from furious Annie Walker. She was engaged to sailor Harry McLean, who returned to the sea when they both decided they did not want to be tied down. In 1978 she married Alf, who threw her uncouth step-father out of the wedding reception when he loudly insinuated that Alf had married Renee for her money. At the time of her death in a car crash, Renee was about to sell the shop and move with Alf to a sub-post office in Grange-over-Sands.

Ena Sharples
VIOLET CARSON

Born: 14.11.1899
Education: Factory School.
Address: Retired to Lytham St Annes.

Battling Ena, with her hairnet clamped on her bulldog head like a tin helmet, would take on anyone in authority. She had a healthy distrust of all politicians, and an undying respect for Royalty. As the Street's self-appointed watch committee, she sat in judgement in the Rovers' Snug, passing vinegar-tongued opinions on everything and everyone.

Ena – big, bossy and brusque – had a hard life and was a graduate of the school of hard knocks. She was critical of her friends, but loyal, and an occasional act of kindness revealed the gentler side she kept well hidden. She began work at eight as a piecer in Hargreaves Mill, and graduated to operating a loom. In World War I she was a tram conductress, and returned to the mill in 1925. From the age of sixteen Ena carried a scar on her left knee, a memento of the time she fell from her bicycle when her handlebars locked with Albert Tatlock's on a ride up Rivington Pike.

She lived in Inkerman Street before moving to the Glad Tidings Mission as caretaker when her husband Alfred died. They had three children – Vera, who died at forty-six, Madge who emigrated, and Baby Ian, known as 'Half-pint', who only lived four days.

Ena, as tough as a mill cog, was buried alive when a train crashed over the Viaduct in 1967. She suffered concussion and a broken arm, but discharged herself from hospital after a week. Whenever she needed a rest she would visit wealthy Henry Foster in St Annes, for whom she kept house from time to time. She now lives there in retirement.

Percy Sugden (Bill Waddington)

Percy Sugden
BILL WADDINGTON

Born: 8.4.1922
Education: Weatherfield Elementary School.
Address: Community Centre, Coronation Street.

   Widower Percy trained as a commis chef at the Grand Hotel and served in the Royal Army Catering Corps, but some people can only take him in small helpings. Pompous Percy, the Community Centre caretaker, loves power – give him a little authority and he visibly grows six inches. He cleared the road for Len Fairclough's funeral, acted as the Street's unpaid policeman, organized his niece's wedding cars, and threatened to take Fred Gee to the Lord Chief Justice for the way he ran the Rovers' raffle. As the Town Hall jobsworth he even tried to book council chief Alf Roberts for parking.

   Percy secretly fancies Emily Bishop and was miffed when Curly Watts moved in as her lodger. His companion is an overbearing budgie called Randy who almost gave Mavis Riley a nervous breakdown by living up to his name with her pet budgie Harriet.

Dave Smith
REGINALD MARSH

   Jaunty Dave Smith, with his trilby always cocked at a racy angle, was the Street's bookie. He was a sharp dealer who would double-cross anyone – but he had a soft heart too. When Hilda's son-in-law died in Australia, Dave lent her £600 to bring her daughter home. Dapper Dave had an eye for the ladies, and now lives with Blanche Hunt at his Kennilworth country club.

Jed Stone
KENNETH COPE

Born: 6.3.1940
Education: Liverpool Council Schools. Borstal.

   The Scouse tearaway with the heart of gold lodged with Minnie Caldwell and turned his hand to anything, as long as it was crooked. His business deals ranged from fruit machines to selling waxworks dummies, and the law finally caught up with him when he was jailed for receiving stolen blankets. Present whereabouts unknown, but the police would probably like to talk to him.

Jed Stone (Kenneth Cope)

Leonard Swindley
ARTHUR LOWE

The testy, teetotal lay preacher of the Glad Tidings Mission told Ena Sharples to mend her ways when he caught her with a milk stout in the Rovers. Pompous Mr Swindley saw himself as a pillar of the community. He founded the Property Owners and Small Traders Party – and finished bottom of the poll. He was fussy and officious, and only Miss Nugent saw his good side. They planned to marry, but the wedding was called off on the day. Mr Swindley ran Gamma Garments for the mysterious Spiros Papagopolous, who recalled him to head office in 1969.

Dennis Tanner
PHILIP LOWRIE

Born: 1.4.1942
Education: Bessie Street Schools.
Address: Thought to be living in London.

Elsie's optimistic son Dennis had a knack for getting into trouble. Nagged by his mother into finding a job, he launched into a bizarre career on the fringe of showbiz. It led him to take a chimp as a lodger, keep a performing sea-lion in the bath and fall for a stripper who used a snake in her act. Somewhere there was a fortune waiting to be made – but hapless Dennis never found it. He tried ladies' hairdressing, selling novelties, even launching himself as rock singer Ricky Dennis.

The Street's most lovable loser married Cockney Jenny Sutton and left Weatherfield in 1967. He was last heard of in Wormwood Scrubs serving three years for breaking and entering, and is now thought to be working on his latest plan to make a million somewhere in London.

Elsie Tanner
PAT PHOENIX

Born: 5.3.1923
Education: Bessie Street Schools.
Address: Gregory's Bar, Algarve, Portugal.

Elsie, three times married, was the Street's sex symbol for many years until some unhappy affairs made her take stock of the passage of time. Fiery-haired, with a temper to match, she would wade into battle with her hand on her hip and finger wagging. Elsie's earthy sophistication and a fondness for gin, her favourite tipple, gave her the veneer of a woman of the world. But she had a soft-spot for young lovers, and often gave her lodgers good advice and a shoulder to cry on. Her own love-life was cratered with disappointment, but she always presented a fully made-up face in public.

Her first marriage, to Arnold Tanner when she was sixteen, lasted twenty-two years. They had a wayward son, Dennis, whose get-rich-quick schemes often ended in disaster, and a daughter, Linda. An old wartime sweetheart, US Army Sergeant Steve Tanner, walked back into her life, and they married in 1967. Both realized that they had tried to breathe life into a dream, and they drifted apart. Steve was murdered by another soldier a year later.

Elsie turned down two proposals from Len Fairclough, and retained a unique understanding of him – which did not please his wife Rita. Her third marriage, to Alan Howard, broke up and Elsie moved to Torquay for a while with her new flame, chauffeur Ron Mather.

Her jobs almost outnumbered her men – from Miami Modes to Gamma Garments, the Posy Bowl, Sylvia's Separates and Baldwin's Casuals. In 1984 Elsie sold No. 11 and flew to Portugal to live with an old lover, Bill Gregory. She is still there, sunning herself with one eye on the beach romeos, and the other on the wrinkles.

Steve Tanner
PAUL MAXWELL

Born: 30.10.1924
Died: 25.9.1968
Education: Night school, Boston. Military Academy, West Point.

US Army Master Sergeant Steve Tanner was the wartime GI who won Elsie Tanner's heart. Twenty years later, still in uniform, he walked back into her life and rekindled the flame. Steve was a smooth-talking soldier with Hollywood looks, but soon after their marriage at St Stephen's Methodist Church, Warrington, they both realized they were trying to relive a dream. Steve, Elsie's second husband, was killed falling down a flight of stairs during a fight.

Steve Tanner (Paul Maxwell)

Albert Tatlock
JACK HOWARTH

Born: 10.8.1895
Died: 13.5.1984
Education: Hardcastle's Factory School.

Grumpy Albert was born in Rosamund Street into a family of weavers. He started his education at a factory school, paying tuppence a week, and working part-time at the mill when he was eight years old. With his flat cap and toothbrush moustache, he was a regular at the Rovers counting his coppers and trying to cadge a rum if someone was buying a round. Albert looked at the world with a jaundiced eye, and only seemed happy when he visited Ken Barlow's twins in Glasgow.

The war featured heavily in Albert's memories, and he even refused to ride in Ken's Volkswagen Beetle because it was a 'Jerry car'. He voluteered for the army months before the outbreak of World War I and fought at the Somme. After a couple of rums his favourite topic of conversation was always Vimy Ridge or Flers Courcelette. Albert was awarded the Military Medal as a Lance Corporal, but would never say why.

After the war he married Bessie Vickery and returned to Hargreaves Mill. His wife gave birth to their daughter Beattie when he was unemployed during the Depression. In 1933 he became full-time steward of Weatherfield Labour Club, and in World War II worked as a temporary clerk at the Town Hall until his retirement.

No. 1 Coronation Street was his home from 1919. His daughter married and moved away in 1953, and his wife died six years later. Albert's niece Valerie lived with him until she married Ken in 1962. She died in 1971, but he still regarded Ken as 'family'.

Albert almost remarried three times. Widow Clara Midgeley proposed to him in 1965, but they both agreed that it would not work out. In 1969 he got as far as the altar with widow Alice Pickens, but the vicar was delayed, so they decided to call it off. Albert proposed to Minnie Caldwell in 1973, thinking they might be better off on a joint pension. When the awesome thought of his full marital obligations dawned on him, he hurriedly called it off. Albert, former lollipop man, and curator of his regimental museum, died in 1984 while staying with Beattie in Cumberland Close, Weatherfield.

Bert Tilsley
PETER DUDLEY

Born: 8.6.1935
Died: 16.1.1984
Education: Rochdale Road Elementary School.
Night school engineering course, Weatherfield Tech.

  Easy-going Bert let his wife do all the shouting, but his strength of character surfaced when he thought there was a principle worth defending. He was fond of classical music and astronomy. But as opportunities were limited in the Street, he spent most of his spare time at home. Bert was handy at home improvements, but seldom made a start unless Ivy nagged him into it. He was once a keen snooker player, until she complained that he thought more of watching Hurricane Higgins than talking to her, so he uncomplainingly gave it up. Bert never fully recovered from a garage explosion and had a mental breakdown. He died in hospital near Southport in 1984.

Ivy Tilsley
LYNNE PERRIE

Born: 8.4.1936
Education: Bessie Street Schools.
Address: 5 Coronation Street.

  Ivy is an abrasive little Lancashire lady with strong trade union loyalties. She loves to champion the underdog, but is shrewd enough to always make sure she is on the winning side. When Hilda Ogden was sacked from the factory for wilful damage to her brush, shop steward Ivy called a walk-out to demand her reinstatement – even though Hilda was not in the union. At home she liked to rule the roost, but her late husband Bert would put her in her place when she interfered too much in Brian's life. Bert's death was a loss for Ivy, but she still has the girls to boss at Baldwin's Casuals.

Brian Tilsley
CHRISTOPHER QUINTEN

Born: 15.10.1958
Education: Hardcastle's Factory School and
Weatherfield Technical College.
Address: 5 Coronation Street.

The Street's brash, muscular motor-bike fanatic
who settled down, but still has a wild streak
simmering beneath the married man. Gail Potter
became his steady girlfriend, and unsteady pillion
passenger. When they fell out over his obsession
with bikes, Brian reluctantly parted company
with his Triumph Bonneville 750 and bought a
car. Their marriage brought family trouble
because Gail was not a Catholic. Brian and Gail
bought a new 'micro-bijou' house, but Gail felt
unsettled when he took a job in the Middle East,
leaving her alone with baby Nicky. Since he came
home, their marriage has become stronger,
despite setbacks. They sold the house in Buxton
Close to keep the garage going, and Brian works
hard to build the business up with the help of two
mechanics.

Gail Tilsley
HELEN WORTH

Born: 18.4.1950
Education: Weatherfield Girls School. Two
O-levels.
Address: 5 Coronation Street.

Marriage to Brian brought Gail the security she
missed as a child. She was illegitimate, and never
knew her father. Her flighty mother Audrey never
had a steady job. Gail arrived in the Street with
her friend Tricia Hopkins to work at the Mark
Brittain Warehouse in 1974. When the Warehouse
burned down she moved to Sylvia's Separates,
and was shocked to find herself cited in a divorce
by the wife of a thirty-five-year-old man she had
known only briefly.

Gail wants to give her family all the things she
missed. She has a quiet but iron determination,
and pushed Brian to take the plunge into business
on his own. She has her differences with his
mother Ivy, but they have much in common when
it comes to stubbornness and a drive to see him
succeed. Her son Nicky goes to playschool while
Gail works full-time running Jim's Cafe in
Rosamund Street.

Betty Turpin
BETTY DRIVER

Born: 4.2.1920
Education: Clackers Lane Elementary and Senior Schools.
Address: 37 Hillside Crescent, Town Lane, Weatherfield.

Bossy Betty, the Rovers buxom barmaid, has an ear for gossip almost as keen as Hilda Ogden's. If someone appears when Betty is talking about them, she breaks into a cracked smile, and switches to a scowl almost before their back is turned. Betty became barmaid of the Rovers in 1969 and has been a cornerstone of the pub ever since. She has rowed with everyone who has been in charge of the bar, and regulars give her a wide berth when her temper is up. Betty was married to police sergeant Cyril Turpin, who died in 1974. Her illegitimate son Gordon was brought up by her sister Maggie. When the truth became public Betty felt ashamed, but was surprised to find that no one was interested. Despite her failings, she still pulls the best pint in Weatherfield.

Annie Walker
DORIS SPEED

Born: 11.8.1909
Education: Clitheroe Council School.
Address: 20 Peacock Terrace, Derby.

Weatherfield's First Lady ruled the Rovers Return with a dignity born of years ministering to the working classes. Although she was the product of an elementary education, Annie believed that the reason she was not selected for grammar school was entirely due to an incompetent education authority. She regarded herself as an intellectual, and able to converse as an equal with Ken Barlow. As a Beaumont of Clitheroe she looked down on her neighbours in tolerant superiority, but with occasional evidence of a deep understanding of human nature. Annie began her working life in a cotton mill, but managed to keep it very quiet.

As a member of Clitheroe Amateur Operatic Society in the 1930s, she insisted on taking a leading role in the occasional productions staged by the Street's Dramatic Society. Her last appearance was as Lady Bracknell in *The Importance of Being Ernest*, but she will always consider herself a thespian. In 1937 she married Jack and moved to the Rovers. He tolerated her whims and fancies and, despite her constant accusation that he was devoid of ambition, they understood each other and managed to live in harmony.

In 1973 widower Alf Roberts invited her to become Mayoress of Weatherfield, and she fulfilled her office with almost regal dignity and charm. The role inspired her to buy a second-hand Rover 2000, a vehicle most suited to her lifestyle. Annie has now given up the licensed trade and lives with her daughter Joan, who did well for herself and married a teacher.

Billy Walker
KENNETH FARRINGTON

Born: 8.9.1938
Education: Mrs Dudley Henderson's Private
School (expelled for fighting). Bessie Street
Schools. Evening classes, Weatherfield Tech.
Address: Now living in Jersey.

Billy turned up periodically at the Rovers like
the proverbial bad penny. When he left, early in
1985, he severed almost half a century of family
connections with the pub. Billy was usually
involved in suspect deals, and under his care, the
Rovers became known for late-night drinking
sessions.

He had a long list of girlfriends, most of whom
Annie strongly disapproved. He was on the brink
of marriage four times, on one occasion to
Deirdre Barlow before she met Ken. His shady
money schemes landed him in trouble and finally
cost him the Rovers. Newton and Ridley
manoeuvred him into giving up the licence when
he was suspected of selling his own supermarket
spirits instead of the brewery's. Billy left by night
to an uncertain future in Jersey, where he once
managed an hotel.

Jack Walker
ARTHUR LESLIE

Born: 26.4.1901
Died: 8.7.1970
Education: Local primary and senior schools.

Cheery, easy-going Jack was the Rovers' popular landlord and a good listener to his customers' troubles. The whole Street mourned his death in 1970. He built up a loyal crowd of regulars, in spite of Annie's attempts to drag the place, protesting, up-market with a Cocktail Hour. Long-suffering Jack, sleeves rolled up, would listen patiently to her latest scheme for social improvement and sigh. His lip-service was a character lesson in self control. Jack died suddenly on a visit to his daughter Joan in Derby.

Curly Watts
KEVIN KENNEDY

Born: 4.7.1963
Education: Grammar school, eight O levels, two A-levels.
Address: 3 Coronation Street.

Curly – real name Norman – squints at the world through lemonade bottle lenses, but has a shrewd mathematical mind. He turned down university to become a binman because he needed the money. Curly's main interest is astronomy. He also has an eye for the girls, but little success. Sharon Gaskell at the Kabin raised his hopes when she asked for a date, but only wanted him to carry her bags to the station. Curly is only calculating when it comes to sums – he once worked out racing tips for Chalkie Whiteley, and won him £3,500. With girls he is slow at putting two and two together.

In his private moments Curly enjoys literature. He was annoyed when Eddie Yeats did not pick him as best man for his wedding – he had already written the speech, complete with quotations from Shaw and W.B. Yeats.

Bill Webster
PETER ARMITAGE

Elaine Webster
JULIE GRIDLEY

Debbie Webster
SUE DEVANEY

Kevin Webster
MICHAEL LE VELL

Property repair man Bill breezed into the street with daughter Debbie and son Kevin to buy No. 11 for £10,000. Happy-go-lucky Bill was an understanding father who kept his rare bursts of temper for the neighbours. He had rows in the street while settling in, but mellowed when he met Percy Sugden's niece Elaine. Cheeky Debbie took to her, but Kevin was upset by the romance. When the family moved to Southampton, he sulked and stubbornly refused to follow them. He patched up differences with his father, and the break made him more outgoing and independent.

Chalkie Whiteley
TEDDY TURNER

Binman Chalkie bought Len Fairclough's old house, No. 9, for £10,000 and moved in with his drum-playing grandson Craig. Awkward Chalkie annoyed Len by refusing to redirect his mail, and insisting that he repaired the boiler. A neighbours' feud loomed, but Chalkie's good nature won through and they buried their differences. His biggest headache was not Len, but domineering Phyllis Pearce. All Chalkie wanted was peace, but there was no escape from bossy Phyllis. When Craig emigrated to Australia, Chalkie fell ill and suffered under her ministrations. Exhausted from an overdose of Phyllis, he put his house up for sale and followed Craig to Australia in 1983 with the help of a £3,500 win on the horses. His parting shot was to give Phyllis only £30 from the winnings – to ensure she did not follow him.

Eddie Yeats

GEOFFREY HUGHES

Born: 22.8.1941
Education: Liverpool Council Schools. Borstal.
Address: 12 Silk Street, Bury.

Eddie, the roly-poly Scouse binman with the soft heart, arrived in the Street in 1974 on parole from Walton Jail. He fancied Bet Lynch, and cheered her up when she was close to suicide after her son's death. Stan became his window-cleaning partner, but Eddie's criminal past caught up with him. He used the round to pick targets for his burglar mates. Despite another six-month jail sentence, Eddie still felt hurt when people refused to believe he was going straight. He lodged with Stan and Hilda who treated him like a son, and he often took Hilda's side in badgering Stan to work. Good-natured Eddie was fond of them, and never really minded Stan's cadging.

As a Weatherfield binman, he met his future wife Marion, and gave her a carpet for their bottom drawer. Marion was delighted – until she realized someone had thrown it out. After the wedding Eddie asked for a transfer to Bury Refuse Department so that his wife could nurse her sick mother.

Marion Yeats

VERONICA DORAN

Born: 18.12.1950
Education: Bury Council School.
Address: 12 Silk Street, Bury.

Eddie's toothy wife Marion was a CB radio fan with the handle 'Stardust Lil'. They were both keen breakers, but off the air had problems finding somewhere quiet to do their courting. Eddie was stunned when Marion told him she was pregnant, but when she saw that he was pleased she was overjoyed. After the honeymoon in Benidorm, she learned that her mother had suffered a stroke. Marion offered to look after her, but wept because her married life was not starting the way she had dreamed. They have both settled happily in Bury with a family of their own.

How Coronation Street was born

Stuart Latham, *Coronation Street's* first producer, recalls the original live transmission and the subsequent success . . .

In 1960 a young and stage-struck member of Granada's office staff submitted an idea for a thirteen-part serial of daily life in a street of terraced back-to-back houses in a typical Salford community. The young man was Tony Warren, sole creator of Ena Sharples, Elsie Tanner, Mr Tatlock, the Rovers Return public house and Florrie Lindley's Corner Shop

In H.V. Kershaw's entertaining and informative *The Street Where I Live* he generously writes that 'the second name on the *Coronation Street* roll of honour must assuredly be that of Harry (Stuart) Latham, without whom the programme would have lost a great deal of its truth and without doubt most of its life.'

Whether there is any truth in this accolade or not, at the time I was just a freelance director on a twelve-month contract with Granada, doing the work I liked, to the best of my ability, and with complete dedication to the handful of scripts provided by Tony Warren. They were, with the exception of a play which had come my way as director of the famous Armchair Theatre series, of a quality and originality I had not had the good fortune to encounter before in commercial television.

Denis Forman – at the time Programme Controller for Granada, now Sir Denis and Chairman of Granada Television – described my attitude with his customary accuracy as one of 'mutinous loyalty'. The loyalty was directed to the most complete realization of Tony's conception we could achieve, and the 'mutiny' to any of the top brass from Cecil Bernstein down who came – with however good intentions – between my production team and that realization.

I had secured the services of two young staff directors – Mike Scott, who could be relied on for an efficiently professional job, while never seeing his future in such dingy surroundings (he is now Programme Controller for Granada) and Derek Bennett, a fast-learning enthusiast who tackled the job with total commitment. A New Zealander, Eric Price, was the third staff director, While I directed every fourth pair of programmes myself in order to maintain personal contact and control over the cast. Together we made as good

Stuart Latham.

a team as Granada had to offer. The all-important visual side of the Street was fortunately entrusted to Denis Parkin, whose imprint still remains nearly twenty-five years later.

But the problem of casting almost sank the whole operation. That department was metropolitan south in knowledge and imagination. However, we were lucky to have a junior named Jose Scott, who was from the north and knew North Country concert-party and repertory theatre.

Welding a nervous and largely inexperienced company into a working unit for the tight schedule of two half hour programmes a week could never have been done successfully without the unstinted help of the best floor manager, Dick Everitt, and the best stage manager, Sheila Atha, to be had.

Having started as a very young actor and stage manager at Alexandra Palace before ever the first public television programmes in the world were transmitted by the BBC, I had literally grown up in the medium and never suffered the traumatic nerves later generations of new directors seemed to experience. True, live transmission, which was then the order of the day, caused a palpable

Camera rehearsal in Studio 2 for the first episode.

increase in the adrenalin flow, but it was also highly enjoyable – and in drama actors usually gave better performances touched with an indefinable sense of immediacy.

Our original schedule involved intensive rehearsal of two episodes from Monday through Thursday, culminating in a long day on the Friday when both episodes were rehearsed in Granada's smaller Studio 2 on camera in the actual sets. At 7 p.m. the first episode went out live and, after a fifteen-minute respite, the second episode was pre-recorded for the following Monday. It was a gruelling operation for all concerned.

Right up to the eve of the first scheduled transmission I still had two big problems – three if one includes the eleventh-hour casting of Ena Sharples! Firstly it became clear that Tony had temporarily shot his delighted bolt, and the original scripts – hardly four weeks' air time – were just about all we had, or were likely to have,

for a while. Secondly, Sidney Bernstein's diligent viewing of the pilot programmes was warm with approval of everything except the serial's title – 'Florizel Street', 'Jubilee Street', and so on.

The first I solved gratefully by remembering that when I was directing Armchair Theatre for ABC-TV, at Didsbury on the other side of Manchester, we had received two original scripts from a local insurance agent and keen amateur actor, one of which was excellent. So H.V. Kershaw was brought into the team, and Harry remains there to this day. He had already found his way onto the Granada payroll anyway.

The second and more agonizing problem was solved in the New Theatre Tavern late one night after much lonely concentration. It was a matter of euphony – the trisyllabic names were wrong. *Coronation Street* finally appeared in neon lights over a bottle of Haig. I went back to the studios, and I don't think I told anyone my decision that night except the Graphics Department.

The late Eric Spear was suggested by Peter Taylor, then in charge of the Music Department, to provide the theme tune. I am convinced that when Eric came up to Manchester – reluctantly leaving the Channel Islands – to view the early pilots made by Mike and Derek, he already had the world-famous melody as an unsold property. In response to Derek's impassioned spiel about the grainy realism of the project, his main concern (in which he succeeded) was to sell it to us.

In the quarter century since all those early alarums and excusions, inevitably several of the cast have died or left the programme. I still remember with gratitude Arthur Leslie, as Jack Walker the landlord of the Rovers Return, who was at all times a tower of strength in the company, and an oasis of calm common sense when things became fraught – as they have a way of doing in a television studio. And Pat Phoenix, who later graduated as a fully-fledged old-style glamour star, gave unstintingly of her time and energy to rehearse with the less-experienced younger members of the Tanner household.

The highly publicized career of Elsie Tanner symbolizes one of the many threats to the integrity of the Street as did that of Ena Sharples, who became as famous and loved as the Queen Mother, from Australia's Bondi Beach to Blackpool sands. It became harder for the producer and his directors to maintain the low-profile naturalism of the programme. The advent of colour television indirectly added a further challenge to sober realism. The early episodes were in grainy black and white. I am happy to say that all our combined efforts proved successful and *Coronation Street* spread irresistibly to the whole ITV network in a matter of months. I am still amazed that Anglia (Tory yeoman farmers?) and Southern (retired rear-admirals?) succumbed first.

There have been, I think, eighteen producers after me and each has made a distinct contribution. The most difficult job fell to Derek Granger. Although myself a Londoner born and bred, I knew Manchester well having played the old Opera House on tours by London companies several times as a young actor, spending the week in Acker Street famous for its theatrical digs, and later for two years I directed the Library Theatre in St Peter's Square when it opened as a civic theatre. Derek, however, was a journalist and critic from — in my favourite description of him — the Brighton South Coast Literary and Theatrical Mafia.

To him fell the task of steering *Coronation Street*, now covering the whole ITV network and regularly top of the rating charts, through the shoals of muddled criticism from portentous writers belatedly catching up with the phenomenon, and usually trying to explain it away. Some most hilarious reading is to be found in the solemn social treatises of the time, and Granger's sensible and witty ripostes are a joy. No one except Harry Kershaw has written with such lucid sympathy about the baby I left them both holding.

In 1981 the National Film Theatre paid tribute to Granada's coming of age with a number of representative programmes, one of which was made up of the very first four episodes. It sold out immediately it was announced, and a repeat performance had to be hastily organized. I attended the first showing and was fascinated to find that the packed audience had an average age of twenty-five. Not only did they obviously love the evening, but Ena Sharples' famous first scene in Florrie Lindley's shop was greeted with a thunderous round of applause. Here was vintage Tony Warren magic at work. On the way home from the NFT, chuffed by the warmth of the reception, I slowly realized that the audience had, of course, all grown up with the Street twice weekly on the family telly . . . an anchor, a point of reference in a confusing world, a marker. So here's to the next twenty-five years, and continuing success to the longest-serving producer of all, Bill Podmore.

Half an hour of television history – the first episode

Coronation Street was conceived by Salford-born scriptwriter Tony Warren, and delivered into the world on 9 December 1960 by a tiny production team who believed it might run for six months if they were lucky. Its working title was 'Florizel Street', then it almost became 'Jubilee Street' but, after a vote *Coronation Street* prevailed.

Six months earlier Tony Warren, working in Granada TV's Promotion Department, had submitted an idea for a twice-weekly serial. He had toured pubs in Manchester, worked as a barman, talked to people in buses and trains, wandered through street markets and made trips to Blackpool Illuminations to research his theme. The idea was simple – life in a northern, working-class back street.

It has been with us twice a week, every week, ever since. And, mirroring the lives, loves and humour of the millions who watch it avidly, it will probably be around for another twenty-five. We may have beer in cubes and computerized chip pans by then, but Britain will still have legions of Percy Sugdens, bosses like Mike Baldwin, landladies like Bet, cleaners like Hilda and, if we are unlucky, neighbours like the Duckworths.

Tony Warren's original vision remains as unchanged now as it was when it first took shape a quarter of a century ago: 'A fascinating freemasonry, a volume of unwritten rules. These are the driving forces behind life in a working class street in the north of England. The purpose of "Florizel Street" is to examine a community of this nature, and to entertain.'

The name may have changed, but *Coronation Street* has exceeded everyone's expectations, rarely slipping from the top half of the top ten programmes in twenty-five years. That first programme, which went out live at 7 p.m. with Florrie Lindley taking over the Corner Shop from Elsie Lappin who was retiring to a bungalow at Knott End, seems an age away . . .

Young Ken Barlow met his first girlfriend, the rather posh Susan Cunningham. And Elsie Tanner was – not for the first time – urging her layabout son Dennis to get a job. Over the next few weeks wayward Lucille Hewitt turned up on the doorstep of her bus inspector dad, Harry. She had run away from a council home, but returned four days before Christmas.

Ken and Susan caused a stir by taking part in a Ban the Bomb march through Weatherfield. And Linda Cheveski, Elsie's daughter, announced that she was pregnant. Her Czech husband Ivan was away in Birmingham, working as an engineer. The Street had its first death, too. May

The original cast pose for their first picture together.

History in the making – the minutes tick away before the cameras roll! on episode one.

May Hardman collapses – the first death in the Street.

Hardman collapsed from a heart attack at No. 13, the terraced house where Hilda Ogden now lives.

Along with Ena Sharples, Annie Walker, Albert Tatlock and the Barlows, the characters of

Britain's best-loved TV series stepped before the *Coronation Street* cameras for the first time. And this, in full, is the historic first episode of the world's longest-running television show.

'CORONATION STREET'

Episode One

by Tony Warren

Cam. Reh.: Thurs. 8 Dec. 1960. 15.00–18.30 hrs. in Studio Two
X/M:
Fri. 9 Dec. 1960. 19.00–19.30 hrs. in Studio Two

CAST:

Elsie Lappin	Maudie Edwards
Florrie Lindley	Betty Alberge
Linda Cheveski	Anne Cunningham
Elsie Tanner	Patricia Phoenix
Dennis Tanner	Philip Lowrie
Kenneth Barlow	William Roache
Ida Barlow	Noel Dyson
Frank Barlow	Frank Pemberton
David Barlow	Alan Rothwell
Ena Sharples	Violet Carson
Albert Tatlock	Jack Howarth
Susan Cunningham	Patricia Shakesby
Annie Walker	Doris Speed

CREW:

1. Producer	S. Latham
2. Director	D. Bennett
3. Floor Manager	D. Everitt
4. Prod. Asst.	D. Angel
5. Designer	D. Parkin
6. Technical Sup.	R. Hanson
7. Lighting Sup.	K. McCreadie
8. Stage Manager	S. Atha

Ext. Shop Window.
Two girls are playing with a ball and singing. Mrs Lappin comes out of door with boy and operates bubblegum machine for him. She looks up at sign which reads 'Mrs Lappin – Corner Shop' then returns inside.

Studio Int. The General Shop at the corner of Coronation Street.
A counter runs along two sides of the shop. A door at the back of the counter leads into the living quarters.

Mrs Elsie Lappin – a small, birdlike woman with a faintly aggressive manner – is talking with Mrs Florrie Lindley, a kindly woman, large, short-sighted and altogether warmer than Mrs Lappin.
Both women wear white overalls. They are stacking cans on the shelves at the back of the counter.

Mrs Lappin.

Florrie Lindley.

MRS LAPPIN: . . . Now the next thing you want to do is get a signwriter in. That thing above the door'll 'ave to be changed.
FLORRIE: It'll seem funny 'avin' me name outside me own shop. Florrie Lindley, licensed to sell . . .

73

MRS LAPPIN: (Sternly) Florence, you mean.

FLORRIE: Eh?

MRS LAPPIN: Well, that's your real name, isn't it?

FLORRIE: Yes, but nobody uses it. Come to that, I've got another one too.

MRS LAPPIN: That'll 'ave to go up outside then.

FLORRIE: Whatever for?

MRS LAPPIN: (Firmly) It's the law.

FLORRIE: Florence Lena Lindley. It sounds like an embrocation.

MRS LAPPIN: The Patent Medicine man calls Thursdays. Now you've got to watch 'im. 'e could sell sand to the Arabs.

FLORRIE: I'll remember that. There's more to it than you'd think, isn't there?

Florrie takes some cans and begins to stack them in a pyramid shape on the counter.

MRS LAPPIN: You'll soon get into the way of it. (Watching Florrie: almost indignantly) Whatever are you doin' that for?

FLORRIE: I thought it'd encourage folk to buy.

MRS LAPPIN: Well, of course it's up to you now, but it's always been my experience that they come in 'ere with their minds ready made up.

FLORRIE: (Firmly) Well I think it's worth tryin'. At the "Farrier's Arms" the Governor always said that when we 'ung peanuts up behind the bar we got rid of them twice as quick. If you'd waited till folk asked they'd 'ave gone bad on us.

MRS LAPPIN: (Almost snappily: she has not enjoyed the lesson) I wonder you never fancied a pub of your own. I was really surprised when our Sheila first told me you were interested in this.

FLORRIE: You wouldn't get me in no pub of me own. Staff, that's the trouble. No, a little business like this is right up my street, just what I've been lookin' for. Mrs Lappin, I do appreciate your stayin' on while I get into the run of things. You know 'ow it is when you come into a new street. You don't know anyone, you don't know what to look out for.

MRS LAPPIN: Coronation Street's alright. Mind you, there are some you 'ave to watch.

FLORRIE: What 'appens if they ask me for tick?

MRS LAPPIN: Well, I used to 'ave a notice up there: 'Please do not ask for credit as a refusal often offends.'

FLORRIE: Where's it gone?

MRS LAPPIN: They asked just the same. I took it down. It's in the back. No, a bit on the slate's not a bad thing. If you didn't let some of 'em have it they wouldn't spend a quarter as much. Mind you, you 'ave to choose your customer. Now for a start, the Tanners at number Eleven. If you'll take my advice you won't let them go a penny over ten bob. If you do, you won't see sight or sound of 'em from one week's end to another.

FLORRIE: The Tanners from number Eleven. (Dutifully) I'll remember that.

There is a ping as the door opens: Linda Cheveski enters. Linda is twenty-six. She is quite attractive but her figure is better than her face. She knows this and dresses accordingly.

MRS LAPPIN: 'ello Linda. Not gone back then yet?

Linda dumps a shopping bag on the counter and begins to remove empty beer bottles.

LINDA: I've brought you some empties. Oh, and I want a quarter of boiled 'am.
MRS LAPPIN: You've not met Mrs Lindley, 'ave you? This is Linda Cheveski, she married a Pole . . . *(With heavy meaning)* Linda-Tanner-that-was. 'ow's yer mother, love?

Linda Cheveski.

No. 11 Coronation Street.
Int. Over Bannisters.

Elsie follows Dennis downstairs. The Tanners' living room. A door leads onto a corridor. Another door to the scullery. A window looks out onto the yard and backs of other gloomy houses. The room is dominated by black-leaded grate.

Elsie Tanner is arguing fiercely with her son, Dennis. Elsie is in her late forties, with the very battered remains of good looks and figure. Dennis Tanner is in his mid-twenties. He is not particularly good-looking and there is something shifty about him. In conversation his manner verges between the derisive and the defensive.

ELSIE: *(Grimly)* Come on, Dennis Tanner, where is it?
DENNIS: Where's what?
ELSIE: Don't try comin' the innocent with me. You know as well as I do.
DENNIS: I don't know what you're talking about.
ELSIE: Two shillings gone out o' my purse. That's what I'm talking about.
DENNIS: Well, what're you looking at me for? It's nothin' to do with me.
ELSIE: Oh, I suppose some Mayfair cat burglar called in an' nicked it.
DENNIS: Funny eh.

Elsie Tanner.

Dennis Tanner.

Move into kitchen.

ELSIE: Now let's get this straight. Not an hour ago you asked me for two bob for cigarettes.

DENNIS: An' you wouldn't give it me. We know.

ELSIE: *(Indignation boiling)* So you stooped to goin' in a lady's handbag.

DENNIS: Just listen to it. A lady. Is *that* what you crack on you are these days?

ELSIE: *(Grimly)* A fine son . . . a fine son, you are. That judge was right about you. One of these days that tongue of yours'll get you 'ung.

DENNIS: Oh, give over. Look, you've lost two bob. *I* don't know where it is. What am *I* supposed to do about it?

ELSIE: Get work. Get work, that's what you're supposed to do about it.

DENNIS: Oh, change the record, will you.

ELSIE: Did you go down to the Labour today?

DENNIS: I'm not due till tomorrow.

ELSIE: You know what *your* trouble is, don't you? You don't *want* to work. Did you go through the adverts in the papers?

DENNIS: What papers? We only get one in the mornin'. There's nothin' in *that*. You know there isn't.

ELSIE: You could've gone down to the readin' room, couldn't you? 'ere I am workin' myself to death an' you won't even stir yourself to go an' look through a newspaper.

DENNIS: What sort of job would they 'ave for me?

ELSIE: There's jobs for everybody that takes the trouble to look for them.

DENNIS: Yes, an' they ask you what experience you've had.

ELSIE: Well you've got experience.

DENNIS: Not the right kind though. Just drop it will you?

ELSIE: No I won't. It's the same every time I try to talk to . . .

DENNIS: Look, you know as well as I do why I can't get a job.

ELSIE: But you've been out of that place for seven weeks now.

DENNIS: *(Enjoying saying this)* Don't let's wrap it up. If you *mean* prison, say it. *(Bitterly)* Everyone else does.

ELSIE: You can't go on like this.

DENNIS: Well, what am I supposed to do? Just tell me that.

ELSIE: I don't know why it 'ad to be *me* that 'ad to 'ave a son like you.

DENNIS: I suppose you'd rather 'ave me like Kenneth Barlow at number Three. . .

ELSIE: *(Snapping)* An' what's wrong with 'im? I'll tell you something, 'e'll 'ave no trouble gettin' a job. *(Dennis is leaving)* 'e's got plenty in the upper storey an' that's where it counts. *(Sagging)* Yes, I sometimes wish we *were* a bit more like them Barlows at least they're not rowin' all the time.

Barlow's scullery door opening and Ida entering.
The Barlow's living room.

In shape the living room is an exact replica of the Tanner's, but it is better furnished and altogether tidier. A table under the window is set for a meal and the family are eating. Ida Barlow is a kindly woman somewhere in her late forties. Her husband Frank is a little older. Once he might have been muscular but has now gone to seed.
Their son Kenneth is twenty. He has little or no northern accent and looks faintly out of place in these surroundings.

IDA: Sauce Kenneth?

KENNETH: No thank you.

IDA: Oh, and I got it specially. You always *loved* it when you were little.

KENNETH: Did I?

Frank helps himself liberally to the bottled sauce. Kenneth watches and shudders involuntarily. His father looks up and catches his eye.

FRANK: What's up?

KENNETH: *(Looking away)* Nothing.

FRANK: What's that snooty expression for then?

KENNETH: What snooty expression?

77

Ida Barlow.

Ken Barlow.

Frank Barlow.

IDA: *(Hastily to Kenneth)* That new pullover's turned out a treat. I'll never knit another one in that colour though. Navy blue plays the devil with my eyes.

Frank again picks up the sauce bottle and helps himself to more.

KENNETH: *(Thinks aloud)* Oh *no*.
FRANK: Don't they do this at College then? I'll bet they don't eat in their shirt-sleeves either.

KENNETH: What d'you mean?

FRANK: I've been noticin' you lookin' at me.

KENNETH: I don't know what you're talking about.

FRANK: Oh yes you do. *(With grim satisfaction)* We're not good enough for you.

KENNETH: *(Flaring and appealing to his mother)* I never said a word and he starts.

IDA: Look Dad, let's just 'ave one meal in peace for a change.

FRANK: Now you know 'e doesn't like to 'ear you call me 'Dad', it's common.

IDA: Oh, give over the pair of you. My back's at it again somethin' awful.

FRANK: That's what comes of doin' that rotten job. I bet you don't tell your 'igh and mighty friends *that* Kenneth.

KENNETH: What?

FRANK: That your Mother works.

KENNETH: It's no secret. She works in a hotel kitchen. If anyone asked me, of course I'd tell them.

IDA: *(Sharply)* I don't know what's got into you Frank. You're edgy enough for six. What's up with you?

FRANK: Blame me, *I* would, it's 'im. *(With gloomy menace)* 'Why do we 'ave to 'ave the bread ready buttered?'

IDA: Eh?

FRANK: 'e said that yesterday. An' then again tonight; 'Why do we 'ave to 'ave cups of tea with the food?' Well I'll tell you why – I like food swilled down properly, that's why. You want to watch out, Ida, or 'e'll be 'avin' you changin' into an evenin' gown to eat your meals.

This idea pleases Frank who shuts up and chomps happily.

IDA: Just look at that clock. Wherever can *David* 've got to? *(To Kenneth)* Did you go into town this afternoon?

KENNETH: Yes. Oh, I got a record.

IDA: One *I'll* like?

KENNETH: You might. I'm not sure.

IDA: Well, you know *me*. I've always been one for a bit o' good music. We'll put it on when we've washed up and your Dad's 'ad his sleep. If David doesn't hurry up, that chop'll 'ave gone bone-dry in the oven.

KENNETH: *(Slightly hesitantly)* Oh, by the way, I'm going out later on.

IDA: *(Hesitantly)* Are you meeting a girl?

KENNETH: Yes.

IDA: Oh. *(Pause)*

KENNETH: It's just a girl who's in my year.

IDA: The one you got the letter from this morning? Does she come from round 'ere?

KENNETH: Not far away. The other side of town.

IDA: Are you goin' to their 'ouse then?

KENNETH: No. Just into town.

IDA: Whereabouts are you meetin' 'er?

KENNETH: *(After a moment's hesitation)* The Imperial.

FRANK: *(He can't believe his ears)* Where?

KENNETH: The Imperial Hotel.

FRANK: Now listen, Squire, you'd best make your mind up to it because you're not goin' throwin' money away in no Imperial Hotels.

KENNETH: *(Faintly mockingly)* What d'you mean 'No Imperial Hotels'?

79

FRANK: I mean what I say an' don't come correctin' me.
KENNETH: Look, I'm not asking for any money . . .
FRANK: Oh yes, you've got the money but where did it come from?
IDA: *(Wearily)* Frank. Do we 'ave to go through all this?
FRANK: Listen Ida, I'm not 'avin' you workin' in them stinkin' kitchens at the Imperial for 'im to go chuckin' money back at the place as if it grew on trees. It's downright wicked, that's what it is.
IDA: 'e's not goin' spendin' much. Are you love?
FRANK: You'd best make up your mind to it Ken . . . you're not goin' *at all*.

David Barlow enters from the scullery. He is an eighteen-year-old engineering apprentice, bright, cheerful and thoroughly likeable. He is dressed in a donkey jacket, jeans tucked into his socks and heavy shoes. A canvas lunchbag is slung over one shoulder.

David Barlow.

DAVID: Hellow.
IDA: An' what time d'you call this?
DAVID: I 'ad another puncture.
FRANK: *(Mock wearily)* Which one this time?
DAVID: Front. I thought it was just the valve at first.
FRANK: The sooner you get shut of that ruin, the better. The thing's only fit for t'scrap yard.
DAVID: Don't worry. That's just where it's goin' minute I've got enough for the deposit.

IDA: Deposit? What on?
DAVID: *(Calmly)* What do you think on? A motor bike o' course.
IDA: Over my dead body. *(Ida goes into the scullery)*
FRANK: Is it rainin'?
DAVID: It was a minute or two ago. It's just stopped.
FRANK: I'll go out an' 'ave a look at that bike.
DAVID: It's alright, Dad. I'll see to it after.
FRANK: Where's the puncture outfit?
DAVID: In the saddlebag. I've told you though, don't bother about it.

Frank picks up a torch and exits through the scullery.

DAVID: *(To Kenneth)* 'ow're you?
KENNETH: Alright.

Ida's head appears round the scullery door.

IDA: *(Grimly to David)* Do you want gravy?
DAVID: Wouldn't mind.
IDA: You'll 'ave to wait while I've warmed it up then. *(The head disappears)*
DAVID: Somethin' up Ken?
KENNETH: We've just had another set-to.
DAVID: What was it this time?
KENNETH: I let out that I'm supposed to be meetin' a girl at the Imperial.
DAVID: Oh 'eck!
KENNETH: You can imagine what *that* started.

The two brothers exchange a resigned family look.

END OF PART ONE

Public Bar of the Rovers Return.
Annie Walker stands behind the bar polishing glasses.
Kenneth Barlow enters gloomily.

Annie Walker.

ANNIE: 'ello love.
KENNETH: 'lo Mrs Walker.
ANNIE: *(Sarcastically)* Well, you *do* look 'appy.
KENNETH: *(Grinning)* Can I have twenty cigarettes?

Dennis Tanner enters.

ANNIE: Best?
KENNETH: Please.
ANNIE: *(Coolly to Dennis)* Evenin'.
DENNIS: *(Adding up coppers)* 'alf o' mild. *(Annie goes off for beer and cigarettes)* An 'ow's our local genius?
KENNETH: *(Easily)* Alright.
DENNIS: *(Not pleasantly)* I've not seen your name in the paper recently. 'aven't you been winnin' any more scholarships? *(Kenneth smiles uneasily)*
DENNIS: It's alright for some.
KENNETH: What are *you* up to these days?
DENNIS: Damn-all. *(Annie returns with half of mild on a tray and cigarettes)*
ANNIE: *(To Kenneth)* D'you mind 'em in tens?
KENNETH: No that's alright.
ANNIE: *(Handing the cigarettes over)* Four an' a penny.
KENNETH: *(Feeling in his pocket)* Hang on. It's here *somewhere.*
DENNIS: I'll 'ave twenty fags too.
ANNIE: *(Lifting mild from tray)* That'll be four an' sevenpence 'appeny altogether.
DENNIS: *(Sliding coppers across the counter)* That's for the mild. I'll give you for the cigs another time. *(Takes swig)*

ANNIE: I'm afraid you won't.

DENNIS: What's up? Don't you trust me or somethin'?

ANNIE: That's got nothin' to do with it. It's just a rule of the 'ouse.

Kenneth has now placed a ten shilling note on the counter. Annie gathers up the note and the sixpence halfpenny and goes across to the till.

DENNIS: *(A controlled fume)* Rule o' the 'ouse my . . .

KENNETH: *(Quietly)* Here.

He slides a packet of cigarettes in Dennis's direction.

DENNIS: Ta. *(He downs the rest of his drink)* Well it's the Government's money really, isn't it? See you.

He exits.

ANNIE: *(Returning Kenneth's change)* Whatever did you want to go an' do that for? *(Kenneth shrugs)*

ANNIE: You don't want to go wastin' your pity on 'im. It's Elsie I'm sorry for. Some mother's do 'ave 'em.

The Living Room of No. 11.

Elsie is at the looking glass applying compressed powder to her nose. In the background we can hear the noise of children at play.

ELSIE: *(Grimly to her reflection)* Eeeh, you're about ready for the knacker yard, Elsie.

The noise of the children rises to a crescendo and there is an ominous crash. Elsie tears across to the window and bangs for all she's worth.

ELSIE: Go on. Gerrought, geroff, go an' play where you belong. *(We hear an undecipherable child's voice)* What did you say, Christine Farrar. Just wait until I see your mother. *(Linda enters from the hall)* Kids. I'm sick 'n tired of 'em clattering around in me backin'.

LINDA: There's nowhere else for them to play.

ELSIE: Council should do somethin' about it.

LINDA: I wouldn't go sayin' that too loud if I were you. They might go an' turn this into a Play Street an' then where'd you be? *(Slapping parcel on table)* There's your 'am.

ELSIE: 'ow much do I owe you?

LINDA: Nothin'.

ELSIE: Don't be soft. *(Looking round)* Where's me purse?

LINDA: I've told you. You don't owe me anythin'. I took two bob out o'yer purse before I went.

ELSIE: *(Gloomily)* Oh 'ell.

LINDA: What's the matter?

ELSIE: Talk about 'Give a dog a bad name . . .' I 'ave just wrongly accused your little brother *(Almost indignantly)* an' you, *you're* a little Madam, you know. Fancy just goin' in me purse without so much as a by-your-leave.

LINDA: I'd no change. I didn't want to go breakin' into a note.

ELSIE: You could've told 'er to write it down, couldn't you?

LINDA: It was the new woman. I didn't like. *(Wearily)* Mother, I'll *give* you the two bob if that's 'ow you feel about it.

ELSIE: Give over. *(Pause)* I don't know what we're going to do Linda.

LINDA: What about? Our kid? 'ow much 'as 'e done about gettin' a job? I mean 'as 'e been near the Prisoner's Aid yet?

ELSIE: Three of us can't manage on what *I* get.

LINDA: What d'you mean, three of us? I'm only here for a week.

ELSIE: *(Levelly)* Are you?

LINDA: Well . . . yes.

ELSIE: Come on. Out with it. You've left 'im 'aven't you?

LINDA: Well . . . I suppose I 'ave really.

ELSIE: But why?

LINDA: Per'aps I just didn't like being called Mrs Cheveski. 'ow did you find out?

ELSIE: I didn't. I just guessed. What 'appened?

LINDA: *(Shrugging)* We 'ad a bust-up.

ELSIE: What over?

LINDA: I don't know. We've 'ad that many recently. We never *stop* 'aving 'em. He's that moody.

ELSIE: Foreigners are. Are you sure that's all it is?

LINDA: That's all.

ELSIE: You've not been up to anythin' you shouldn't?

LINDA: 'ow do you mean?

ELSIE: Well, you're not a kid any more. It's no secret round 'ere why your Dad left me.

LINDA: Well, it's *me* that's done the leavin' this time. I've left Ivan. I'm not goin' back, Mam.

ELSIE: What will you do?

LINDA: Get a job I suppose.

ELSIE: An' where will you live?

LINDA: Well . . . *(For the first time we see that she is genuinely upset)* . . . I can't go back, Mam, I can't, you don't know what 'e's like when 'e gets one of 'is moods on 'im. You're frightened of what 'e might do.

ELSIE: Are you really set on this? *(Linda nods)* Well, you know you're welcome 'ere but just try and get on with our Dennis. For all I go at 'im, 'e isn't 'avin' it easy. What about your things? Did you bring all your clothes with you?

LINDA: *(After a sniff)* Most of 'em.

ELSIE: Now we know what that dirty-great suitcase was in aid of. You'll 'ave to get a job, you know that, don't you?

LINDA: Anythin' goin' at your place?

ELSIE: Nothin' in our Department. A couple of girls've just walked out of millinery. I'll get on to it in the mornin'. *(Opening ham and sniffing at it)* Well, I suppose we must be grateful for small mercies . . . at least the 'am's not off.

LINDA: Mam?

ELSIE: What?

LINDA: Shall I go blonde?

ELSIE: What y'askin' me for? If you want to go blonde, you'll go blonde, you know you will.

LINDA: Ivan nearly went mad when 'e found a bottle of peroxide I'd bought an' I wouldn't care but it was only to get a mark off me front tooth. You wouldn't think it but 'e's very narrow-minded.

ELSIE: I seem to've 'eard you say that before.

LINDA: When the new short skirts first came in I 'ad to take mine up, inch by inch, on the sly.

ELSIE: Why?

LINDA: So's 'e wouldn't know. 'e said 'e didn't want other fellers starin' at me legs.

ELSIE: They're nothin' all that marvellous.

LINDA: What d'you mean?

ELSIE: Your legs. I'm afraid you've got the Tanner side of the family to thank for them. I'm not tellin' a word of a lie yer Granma Tanner was that bandy she couldn't 've stopped a pig in an entry.

LINDA: Well I'm not bandy. *(Terrible thought: she looks down)* Eh, am I?

ELSIE: Are you flip.

LINDA: No seriously.

ELSIE: I've told you.

LINDA: D'you think there will be a job at your place?

ELSIE: I don't say they'll 'ave you permanent but they're bound to be lookin' for staff for Christmas.

LINDA: An' what do I do after Christmas?

ELSIE: You'll 've 'ad to think things out a bit by then.

LINDA: You think I'll go back to 'im, don't you?

ELSIE: It wouldn't be the first time you've gone back with it. We 'ave been through this before.

LINDA: That's all you know!

ELSIE: All I know is you 'adn't been married three months before you come flyin' back 'ere with all your beddin', a flight of plaster ducks an' a brass companion set . . . that's all I know.

LINDA: It's different this time.

ELSIE: I see.

LINDA: It is, honest.

ELSIE: Alright, shurrup, I'm tryin' t'ave a bit of a read.

LINDA: Mam *(She's going to say something of importance)*

ELSIE: *(Now really irritated)* What!

LINDA: Never mind, it's nothin.

She makes for the door

ELSIE: What?

LINDA: I've told you. Get on with yer paper. It's nothin'.

ELSIE: What did you make of that new woman?

LINDA: The one in the shop?

ELSIE: Yes.

LINDA: She didn't seem to 'ave much to say for herself.

The Interior of the Corner Shop.
Florrie is talking to Mrs Lappin.

FLORRIE: Whatever made you think o' retirin' to Knott End? Bit *bleak* there, isn't it?

MRS LAPPIN: *(Indignantly)* You wouldn't say that if you saw the residential part, it's the last word, an' then, another thing, the property *is* architect-designed.

FLORRIE: Me, I don't think I could ever *take* to a bungalow.

MRS LAPPIN: 'ow d'you mean?

FLORRIE: Not goin' upstairs to bed. Some'ow it'd seem all wrong. Still, I bet it's set you back a bob-or-two, just the same.

MRS LAPPIN: Nobody can say I 'aven't worked for it. Did you bring any tea with you?

FLORRIE: No, I just finished off what I'd got this mornin'. It seemed too daft to go buyin' more when I was comin' to 'ole shop-ful.

MRS LAPPIN: Well, pass us a packet an' I'll go an' put kettle on. *(Florrie hands Mrs Lappin a packet of tea)* Now you'll be alright on your own. They won't *eat* you, you know. *(Mrs Lappin exits)*

Ena Sharples enters.

Ena Sharples.

ENA: *(Solemnly)* I'm Mrs Sharples.
FLORRIE: Very pleased to meet you.
ENA: I'm a neighbour.
FLORRIE: Oh.
ENA: Are you a widder woman?
FLORRIE: Well, yes.
ENA: Thought so. I'm caretaker of the Glad Tidings 'all.
FLORRIE: That's just down the street, isn't it?
ENA: What's *your* place of worship?
FLORRIE: Well, I don't really do very much about it.
ENA: *(Nodding wisely)* Oh yes, C of E.
FLORRIE: I wouldn't say I was anythin' really.

86

ENA: (*As she sits down*) It's like my sister's husband. 'e were made 'ead of the plumbin' in the place where they live. It gave 'er ideas. She said to 'im: 'We're Civic Dignitaries now, we'll 'ave to 'ead for the church.' Within a week they were received, christened and confirmed and wi'in a fortnight *she* were sittin' up all night sewin' surplices. (*Without pausing*) I'll 'ave a packet o' bakin' powder. Where you bein' buried?

FLORRIE: (*Amazed*) I've not given it much thought.

ENA: (*Emphatically*) Well, you *should*. But think on you don't go to that Crematorium (*Indicating*) down there. As the coffin rolls away, they play *Moonlight and Roses*. I spoke to the Superintendent personally an' 'e said: 'That's not *Moonlight and Roses*, that's *Andantina*.' So I said '*Andantina* or no *Andantina*, I'm rolling away to the *Crimond*.' (*Again without pausing, and indicating cakes*) Are those fancies, today's?

FLORRIE: Yes.

ENA: 'alf a dozen, and no eclairs. (*Almost accusingly*) You're from out of Esmerelda Street, aren't you?

FLORRIE: (*Putting cakes from an open baking tray into bag*) That's right.

ENA: Yes, an' aren't you the one that was on the bar at the Farrier for donkeys years?

FLORRIE: Well, I was there a tidy while.

ENA: 'ave you any children?

FLORRIE: No, no I 'aven't.

ENA: Well, you're better off without 'em. Bottle o' bleach. More trouble than they're worth. (*Regarding Florrie balefully*) Esmerelda Street, eh? Very bay winder down there, aren't they? You'll find things a bit different 'ere. There's some peculiar people in this street. 'ave you come across a Mrs Tanner yet?

FLORRIE: I can't say I 'ave.

ENA: (*Happily*) You will. (*Darkly*) Watch 'er. She's a bad 'un.

Elsie Lappin returns.

ENA: (*Wheeling round on Mrs Lappin*) An' while I think about it (*Accusingly*) you owe me an egg.

MRS LAPPIN: Eh?

ENA: One o' them I 'ad this mornin' were off.

MRS LAPPIN: Well, you should a brought it back.

ENA: (*Indignantly*) Brought it back? Why, I 'ad to 'old a pot towel to me nose before I could so much as carry the thing into me backin', but if my word isn't good enough, I'm sure you're welcome to come an' 'ave a smell at me dustbin.

Silently Mrs Lappin places an egg in a bag and hands it to Ena.

ENA: Ta.

Ena heads for the door.

FLORRIE: (*Nervously*) The other things came to three an' four.

ENA: (*Briskly*) Put it ont slate. I'm not thinkin' o' runnin' away. (*Ena exits*)

Elsie raises her eyes at Florrie.

FLORRIE: Ew . . . isn't she morbid.

Fade.

The Barlow's Living Room: Evening.
David's bicycle is upturned on the floor, the carpet is protected by newspapers, Frank is working on the machine. David looks on.

FRANK: *(Blowing through valve)* It's not the valve an' that's for sure.
DAVID: I told you.
FRANK: Where's your pump?
DAVID: At work.
FRANK: What good d'you think it's doin' there?
DAVID: You don't know what it's like there, Dad, you can't leave a thing lyin' round. They'd knock anythin' off. I 'ave to 'ide it. We'd better get that tyre off. I'll get a couple o' spoons.

He goes over to a drawer.

FRANK: 'as . . . er . . . 'as our Ken said anythin' to you? About goin' out tonight I mean?
DAVID: Yep.
FRANK: Imperial 'otel. That lad's got the cheek o' the devil.
DAVID: *(Pleasantly)* It's 'is own life, *isn't* it?
FRANK: *(Not unpleasantly)* That's right, gang up on me, as per usual.
DAVID: I'll just nip up the street an' borrow a pump. Won't be a minute.

He exits via the lobby. Frank scratches his head and looks worried. Ida enters and starts to potter. Long silent pause.

FRANK: Alright. Blame me then.
IDA: Nobody's blamin' anybody.
FRANK: Where's our Ken then?

Ida sits down with her knitting.

IDA: Next door, in Tatlock's.
FRANK: 'e spends more time in old Daddy Tatlock's than 'e does 'ere.
IDA: You leave 'im alone. Mr Tatlock's all right, Mr Tatlock is.
FRANK: *(Now sitting in chair)* Look love. 'ow can I say to the lad now, 'alright Ken you can go', it'd make me look a proper fool. 'e wouldn't think any the better of me for it.
IDA: And what 'appens if he goes whether or not. What sort of fool are you goin' to look then?
FRANK: That lad should learn to live in 'is own class. Silk ties, sixteen shillings, that doesn't come out of 'is grant and don't tell me it does.
IDA: No, I'll tell you straight, it doesn't. I bought it 'im, *and* 'e never asked me to. I'm no martyr Frank, much as you'd like to think it. I just want 'im to 'ave the chance an' 'e's 'avin' the best chance I can give 'im.
FRANK: *(Sighing)* We certainly raised a rum 'un.

Albert Tatlock's Living Room.
Shot of Kenneth sitting in a chair stroking a cat. The room is crammed with Victorian furniture.
Albert – a benign man of solemn charm aged about seventy is sitting by the table arranging coins in a velvet display board.

ALBERT: I know it's no use askin' *you* to take an interest in my collection. *(Kenneth grins)* If I didn't 'ave these and the Choral Society there'd be nothin' for me to do but go down to that Readin' Room wi' all the other

old ruins. I were changin' me library books the other day an' I just looked in for a minute. I 'ad to come away. It really got on top o' me. Nothin' but snufflin' an' pages turnin' over. I felt like shoutin' 'Getta hobby or you'll be dead inside twelve months.' 'ave you seen me new labels? Esther got them typed for me.

Kenneth deposits the cat on the floor and begins to mooch around the room.

KENNETH: Yes, she told me.
ALBERT: You're very quiet.
KENNETH: *(Coming to)* Sorry. I was just thinkin' about somethin'.
ALBERT: Somethin' wrong?
KENNETH: No. Well, not really.
ALBERT: Is it this business of goin' to the Imperial?
KENNETH: Who told you?
ALBERT: Your mother.
KENNETH: It's a bit of a mess, isn't it?
ALBERT: What're you goin' to do about it?
KENNETH: Well, I've got to go. There was a number to ring if I couldn't, but Susan's bound to 've left by now.
ALBERT: Her name's Susan then?
KENNETH: Yes, Susan Cunningham.
ALBERT: Is she . . . a . . . er special sort of friend?
KENNETH: Not particularly. Just a girl who happens to be in my year.
ALBERT: Of course, an' mark you, this is only an idea, you could always go into town an' collect 'er an' bring 'er back 'ere. I think that'd please your mother.

Pause.

KENNETH: It's no good. I couldn't.

ALBERT: You know best.

KENNETH: I just couldn't. You wouldn't understand . . .

ALBERT: *(Calmly)* Thank you.

KENNETH: It's just that well . . . Coronation Street.

ALBERT: Well, what's wrong with it? This is the first time I've heard you talkin' like this.

KENNETH: I've never pretended to Sue, or anybody for that matter, that I came from anywhere else, but I don't much fancy the idea of her actually *seeing* it.

ALBERT: It's got its good points. Think of Ena Sharples. I should think your friend'd lap 'er up.

KENNETH: *(Mimicking Ena wildly)* 'My place o' worship is the Rovers Return. I'll swop brown ale for an 'ymn book *any* day.'

ALBERT: You see.

KENNETH: It's alright *talking* about it but I don't *want* her coming here.

ALBERT: I never thought the day'd come when I'd 'ave to say this but that College 'as turned you into a proper stuck-up little snob Kenneth Barlow.

KENNETH: Oh, that's not true.

ALBERT: Isn't it?

KENNETH: I just haven't explained myself properly. I . . .

We hear the rattle of the back door opening.

ALBERT: Was that me door then?

IDA: *(Out of vision)* 'ello?

ALBERT: Come on in, Ida.

IDA: Is our Kenneth with you Mr Tatlock? *(She enters – slightly agitated – from the scullery)* Oh, there you are. There's a young lady called for you. It's that friend o' yours, the one you're supposed to meet in town, that Susan Cunningham.

Susan Cunningham.

The Barlow's Living Room.

Evening.

FRANK: Mind what you're doin' lad.

Susan Cunningham — a quietly dressed and attractive girl is with Frank and David who are bent over the machine. Frank is trying to get the wheel off.

DAVID: Let me 'ave a go.
SUSAN: Anything *I* can do?
DAVID: *(Handing her the bicycle pump)* 'old this. Thanks 'ere, our boss comes from round your way.
SUSAN: What's his name?
DAVID: Ernie Parrin.
SUSAN: *(Astonished)* Ernest Parrin.
DAVID: Do you know 'im?
SUSAN: *(With a grimace)* Do I not.
DAVID: Shake.

They shake hands ceremoniously.

DAVID: Excuse the oil. I didn't 'ave chance to wash 'em. Me mam was doin' the pots.

Ida and Kenneth appear from the scullery.

IDA: Whatever must you think of us with a bike in the middle of the floor.

Kenneth takes in the scene.

KENNETH: *(Quietly)* Hello Susan.
SUSAN: Hello, Ken.

LONG VIEW OF THE STREET. AFTER SUSAN'S CREDIT MIX TO PHOTO ROOF TOPS.

A walk round Weatherfield

Artist Dave F. Smith created this map of Weatherfield in 1976. The addresses may have changed, but the old home town still looks the same . . .

Coronation Street–
the next twenty-five years

H.V. Kershaw has been part of *Coronation Street*, as a writer and producer, since it began. He was executive producer until 1972, and has since written prolifically for the Street and other major television series . . .

At eight o'clock on the evening of Friday, 9 December 1960, four men gathered in the lounge bar of the Victoria Hotel in central Manchester, intent on anaesthetizing themselves against a possibly cruel world. An hour earlier they had watched, with a blend of proprietary interest and agonizing apprehension, the first episode of a new twice-weekly serial transmitted by Granada Television from their studios a stone's throw

Harry Kershaw.

away. The men were Tony Warren, Harry Elton, Stuart Latham and myself – respectively the serial's deviser, executive producer, producer and editor.

There was, as there tends to be on such occasions, much prophetic talk. But at no time during the originally incisive, and later maudlin, conversation do I recall anyone suggesting that the show might run for as long as a year. That they would be able to watch their creation, in much the same form and heralded by the same opening music, on Monday, 9 December 1985, was of course unthinkable. Had it been suggested, it would have been ridiculed as the product of an

alcoholic hallucination. And yet, on that date, at seven-thirty in the evening, *Coronation Street* celebrates its Silver Jubilee.

Faced with the question 'Can *Coronation Street* run for a further twenty-five years?' it is necessary to examine the reasons why it has already survived one quarter century. Is there, perhaps, a magic ingredient? This is a widely-accepted possibility as there seems, on the surface, to be no practical reason why the show should be so far ahead of its competitors, both in the size of its audience and the warmth of its critical acclaim. If, however, there is such a magical element, no one is yet sure what it is. And because it has proved so difficult to isolate, successive producers have been reluctant to make wholesale changes in case they should chuck the baby out with the bath water.

My own belief as to why the show has been so hugely popular – a belief I have held since the serial first hit the ratings – is based on the fact that *Coronation Street* is a folk opera in praise of, for want of a better phrase, the 'ordinary' people of Britain. Ignored by TV drama until the Street's arrival, it had been impossible for this vast section of the population to identify with the fantasy characters who people the escapist series of the 1950s. Then, suddenly, everything changed. Here in *Coronation Street* were people who lived around the corner, people they knew, loved, hated, pitied and envied. This was *their* saga and they showed their appreciation of this recognition by turning to the show in great numbers, and remaining faithful for over two decades. And because the inherent character of their counterparts in the real world changes very, very slowly indeed, it would be disastrous to change radically the inherent character of the people in our fictional street. The audience may have become a little richer, a little healthier, and rather better informed but, basically, they have the same worries and the same aspirations as they had twenty-five years ago. The car in the garage and the VCR next to the TV set may point to material change but the important factors of life remain the same. Will our Andrea do well in her A-levels? Will I ever get used to sharing a kitchen with his mother? Will dad keep his job in the next shake-up? These same questions will continue to exercise the minds of our viewers well into the next century.

The prophets of the past have always leapt ahead of time. Fifty years ago it was envisaged that, in 1985, mankind would be dressed from head to foot in aluminium foil, whizz around in solar-powered monorails through the crystal towers of Utopia, and send its elected representatives to some galactic parliament. And what happened? Mr Average takes the same lumbering bus to the same old pub, drinks – if he's lucky – the same old beer and chats about his football team, the weather and the price of fags. The technological revolution may have affected our creature comforts, but it has left our egos untouched.

And if technology were ever capable of changing the nature of mankind surely it would have done so during the lifetime of *Coronation Street*, a lifetime which has witnessed the most startling acceleration in technological know-how since the birth of civilization. When the Street first soared into orbit, Yuri Alekseyevitch Gagarin, the first astronaut, was months away from his own launching; computer technology and the microchip were in their infancy and the housewife, far from looking forward to the onrush of feminism, was yearning for the first reliable non-stick saucepan. Yet, when these fantasies became facts mankind barely blinked. Only in one respect was *Coronation Street* affected – by the growth in competition.

In 1960 the viewing public were faced with a simple choice between ITV and the single BBC channel. the BBC at that time, though strong in experience and expertise, had not yet broken free of the Reithian mould. Their attitude was one almost of condescension to the audience, and it was not surprising that the public grasped the opportunity to switch away from the BBC's dress-suited, starchy image to the showbiz brashness of the independent companies. Even after five years of competition the BBC had still not developed any hard-hitting policy. They were inclined to throw up their hands at the first sign of aggression and *Coronation Street* duly reaped the benefit.

Minority interest programmes and third-rate imports were scheduled to compete directly against the Street, and as a result the programme was able to gather its huge band of faithful followers more quickly than the producers could have hoped. But the battle was not always to be so one-sided. With the advent of BBC 2, the iron began to enter the Corporation's soul. ITV programmes now had to contend with two competing channels. Coupled with this, competitiveness sharpened on BBC 1. Tougher attitudes were taken. Bryan Cowgill was brought from the cut throat world of television sport to the controllership of BBC 1, and immediately began to give the Street a run for its money. First runs of *Till Death Us Do Part* and *Steptoe And Son*, their most popular comedies, were scheduled directly against the serial, or, even more damaging, went on the air ten minutes earlier. The audience, split down the middle, cursed the administrators who were denying them the opportunity to watch both of these favourite programmes. But *Coronation Street* held one decisive weapon – its continuity. While the comedies might pose a serious threat during their run on the screen, those runs were only short. After seven, or at most thirteen weeks, they disappeared to be replaced by less popular shows whilst the Street went on . . . and on . . . and on.

The advent of Channel Four, potentially a

The cameras roll at the Corner Shop – one of the Street's familiar landmarks which millions tune in to see.

much more potent threat than BBC 2, failed to disturb *Coronation Street*'s hold on the viewing public. In the week before Christmas 1984 its lead over the top BBC 1 show was more than five million, and over the top shows on BBC 2 and Channel Four, nine million. So much for past opposition, but what of the future?

The next two-and-a-half decades will undoubtedly offer the viewer a far wider choice of programmes. Cable and, to a larger extent, satellite TV will swamp the airwaves not only with minority programmes of all kinds, but with light entertainment, drama and sport from all over the world (who would have imagined in 1960 that Channel Four would televise the whole of the American Superbowl Final of 1985 live from California?) in addition to the four channel output we already enjoy. How will *Coronation Street* cope with this welter of opposition? My guess is – very well. The show may lose a few peripheral viewers but the vast majority, knowing that they can at best only watch one channel and tape another at any one time, will plump for those shows which they already hold close to their hearts. The British audience is by no means as fickle as some cynics would have us believe. But their loyalty is not unshakable. Take away their favourite elements from any programme and they will drop that programme like a hot potato.

One criticism which has been levelled at *Coronation Street* is that it has lost touch with permissive reality in that its dialogue is not splattered with the coarse language wich forms too large a part of too many lazy vocabularies in the 1980s. It must be recorded that this criticism emanates mainly from the profession (who should know better) and not from the audience. During my long association with the show I have never received a single letter from a viewer complaining about the lack of bad language. Indeed this lack (which, if the show is properly written is unnoticeable) is another major reason for the programme's success. Contemporary drama programmes which neither embarrass nor offend any of their viewers, or fail even to attract part of their potential audience because of pre-publicity which hints at possible embarrassment or offence, are extremely thin on the ground.

Many television producers believe the world to be an extension of their own uninhibited and 'enlightened' milieu and, in producing the programmes they do, give more and more ammunition to the Mary Whitehouses of this world. *Coronation Street* has never entered this arena. Successive producers have been content to feel that mum, dad, the kids and mother-in-law can sit down together and enjoy every episode without feeling the need to switch off, or send the kids out of the room. This is regarded in some professional circles as reactionary. I would only say to those critics that the Street is, and always has been in the business of entertaining people and not of offending them. And if it wishes to stay in that business for another quarter century it must stick to that principle.

It would seem that all the lethal enemies of *Coronation Street* have already done their worst and failed. The question 'Is *Coronation Street* only as strong as its leading characters?' was answered in 1983–84 when the show lost Elsie Tanner, Len Fairclough and Eddie Yeats and suffered the deaths of Jack Howarth, Bernard Youens and Peter Dudley during a period when every week seemed to deal the show a knock-out blow. Yet the serial's hold on the public grew stronger. Nor will we, as long as there is life on earth, ever run out of material. As long as the show remains unpretentious; as long as it continues to amuse, to sadden and to interest a family audience; as long as the artists, the writers and the producers remain as fiercely protective and as proud of their creation as they have been in the past; there is no reason why, in the year 2010, some future chronicler should not be seeking to explain precisely how this phenomenon came to celebrate its Golden Jubilee.

On the street where they live...

Over the years – like any other place in Britain – families and familiar faces have moved in and out of Coronation Street, leaving a store of memories. Behind the drawn lace curtains there have been marriage rows and marriage vows, the rustle of chip shop dinners, raised hopes, tales of tragedy and those touches of northern humour that make the world go round. Here, house by house, is the history of the most famous street in the country:

Rovers Return

Tel: Weatherfield 715 2271
1930–37 George and Elsie Diggins.
1937 Jack and Annie Walker moved in.
1938 Billy Walker was born and, two years later, his sister Joan.
1970 Jack Walker died, leaving Annie to take over the licence.
1984 Annie retired on 8 August. Fred Gee manned the pumps until Billy Walker returned.
1984 December – Billy left and relief manager Gordon Lewis moved in for two weeks. Temporary manager Frank Harvey then took over until . . .
1985 Bet Lynch was appointed manager on 4 February.

Number 1

Tel: 715 8827
Present Occupants: Ken and Deirdre Barlow and Tracey.
Previous Occupants:
1920 Albert Tatlock until his death in 1984.
1960–61 Albert's niece Valerie Tatlock (later Barlow).
1972 Ken Barlow.
1981 Deirdre married Ken, and she and Tracey moved in.

Coronation Street, Rovers Return.

Number 3

Tel: 715 5417
Present Occupants: Emily Bishop and Curly Watts.
Previous Occupants:
1939 Frank and Ida Barlow and their son Ken.
1942 David Barlow born.
1961 Ida was killed in a road accident.
1963 Frank moved to Bramhall, leaving the house empty.

1964 Squatters Betty Lawson and her sons Clifford and Ronnie moved in.
1968–70 Audrey and Dickie Fleming.
1971 Ken Barlow rented the house from Audrey after his wife Valerie's death.
1972 Ken handed the keys over to Ernest and Emily Bishop.

Number 5

Tel: 715 4329
Present Occupants: Ivy Tilsley, Brian and Gail Tilsley and young Nicky.
Previous Occupants:
1961–75 Minnie Caldwell.
1976 Mike Baldwin, accompanied for a short time by Bet Lynch.
1976 Ray and Deirdre Langton and baby Tracey. Ray left his wife and daughter in 1978.
1979 Bert and Ivy Tilsley and their son Brian.
1984 Bert died. Brian, Gail and Nicky moved out to a new 'micro-bijou' house in Buxton Close, but later returned to live with Ivy.

Number 7

Tel: 715 8832
Present Occupant: Rita Fairclough.
Previous Occupants:
1949–63 Harry Hewitt.
1960 Harry's daughter Lucille moved in with him.
1961 Harry's new wife Concepta joined them.
1964 Empty – the Hewitts moved to Ireland.
1965 The house collapsed and was demolished. Len Fairclough rebuilt it and lived there with Rita until his death in December 1983.

Number 9

Tel: 715 8436
Present Occupants: Jack and Vera Duckworth, Terry Duckworth.
Previous Occupants:
1961 Ivan and Linda Cheveski.
1962 Ken and Valerie Barlow. Ken had the house converted into a hairdressing salon for Val.
1965 Twins Susan and Peter born.
1968 The Barlows moved to the new flats and Len Fairclough purchased the house for £1,000. Ray Langton and Jerry Booth lodged with him until 1975.
1977 Rita Littlewood moved in as the new Mrs Fairclough.
1982 Foster daughter Sharon Gaskell joined them.
1982 August, the Faircloughs moved to No. 7 and sold the house to Chalkie Whiteley and his grandson Craig.
1983 Chalkie emigrated to Australia and the Duckworths took over.

Number 11

Tel: 715 8825
Present Occupants: Harry and Connie Clayton and daughters Andrea and Sue.
Previous Occupants:
1939–73 Elsie Tanner.
1940 Linda Tanner was born.
1942 Dennis Tanner entered the world.
1958 Linda left home to marry Ivan Cheveski.
1967 Dennis moved out.
1973–76 Ken Barlow and Janet Barlow.
1976 Elsie returned.
1976–79 Lodger Gail Potter.
1977–79 Lodger Suzie Birchall.
1983 Suzie returned for three months.
1984 Linda Cheveski moved in for three months, before Elsie sold-up and flew to Portugal.
1984 The Websters.
1985 The Claytons bought the house in January.

The Corner Shop.

Number 13

No telephone.
Present Occupant: Hilda Ogden.
Previous Occupants:
1918–60 May Hardman.
1939–62 Daughter Christine Hardman.
1962–64 Jerry and Myra Booth.
1964 Stan Ogden bought the house for £575 and moved in with Hilda and their children Irma and Trevor.
1980–83 Lodger Eddie Yeats.
1984 Stan died.
1985 Lodger Henry Wakefield.

Number 15 – Corner Shop

Tel: 715 7217
Present Occupant: Alf Roberts.
Previous Occupants:
1918–60 Elsie Lappin.
1960–64 Florrie Lindley.
1964 Lionel Petty and his daughter Sandra.
1965 David and Irma Barlow.
1968 Leslie and Maggie Clegg and their son Gordon.
1970–72 Maggie divorced Leslie and went into partnership with Irma Ogden.
1972–74 Irma emigrated to Canada and resident assistant Norma Ford moved in.
1975–76 The Hopkins – Granny Megan, Idris, Vera and Tricia.
1976 Blanche Hunt.
1977 Renee Bradshaw, who married Alf Roberts in 1978, took over and was killed in a road accident in 1980.

Community Centre

Built 1972
1972–74 Resident caretaker: Ena Sharples.
1974–75 Gertie Robson.
1975–80 Ena Sharples as non-resident caretaker.
1981 Eunice and Fred Gee.
1983 Permanent resident caretaker: Percy Sugden.
Community Development Officer: Ken Barlow – he was asked to resign in 1983 when certain council documents were leaked.

Baldwins Casuals.

Baldwins Casuals

1950 Opened as Ellistons Raincoat Factory.
1968 Demolished and luxury flats built on the site.
1971 Flats pulled down because of structural faults which caused the death of Valerie Barlow.
1972 Mark Brittain Warehouse built.
1975 Warehouse destroyed by fire.
1976 Baldwins Casuals opened under proprietor Mike Baldwin. The staff included Vera Duckworth, Emily Bishop, Ivy Tilsley, Shirley Armitage and Ida Clough.

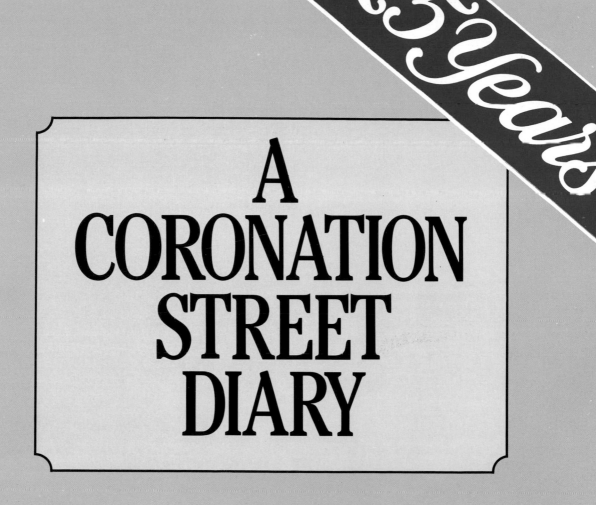

A
CORONATION
STREET
DIARY

25 Years

JANUARY

Teetotal Leonard Swindley, lay preacher at the Glad Tidings Mission, stumbles upon caretaker Ena Sharples quietly enjoying a milk stout in the Rovers Return. Ena indignantly claims it is for medicinal purposes, but the anxiety brings on a stroke. She collapses in the Vestry and is taken to Weatherfield Hospital.

At No. 1, meanwhile, Albert Tatlock is found on his kitchen floor, suffering from high blood pressure. He stubbornly refuses to move in with his daughter Beattie. Roving merchant seaman Arnold Tanner calls on his wife Elsie, who agrees to a divorce.

FEBRUARY

A fractured gas main is found outside the Rovers. PC 'Bobby' Hartley raises the alarm and evacuates everyone to the Mission for the night. Ena strongly objects, but is overruled by Leonard Swindley. Disgruntled, she orders no smoking, talking or 'funny business' – and lights out in the dormitory.

Rovers landlord Jack Walker takes his bowls bag for safe-keeping, and finds his old wartime love letters to Annie. Martha Longhurst later finds one behind a radiator and wrongly accuses Annie of having a secret lover.

MARCH

Ena misreads a notice outside Weatherfield Town Hall and starts a rumour that Coronation Street is to be demolished. The Street's first wedding: Jack and Annie Walker's daughter Joan marries teacher Gordon Davies. Annie is pleased she has done well for herself – Jack is unhappy at the prospect of a teetotal, vegetarian son-in-law.

But as one door opens . . . Ken Barlow ends his affair with middle class Susan Cunningham, explaining that their backgrounds are worlds apart.

APRIL

The Street sends Ena to Coventry for rumour-mongering. She sprains her ankle and moves into 7 Mawdesley Street with widow Martha Longhurst. Ivan and Linda Cheveski buy No. 9 for £565. Ken Barlow has an affair with an older woman – university librarian Marion Lund is thirty-three, Ken is twenty-one.

Rovers regulars take a coach trip to Windermere. Elsie invites rugged Detective Inspector Arthur Dewhurst, whom she had found beaten up outside her back-yard gate. Lucille Hewitt returns to her father, and his widowed sister Alice Burgess agrees to keep house for them.

MAY

Ena is back at the Mission with a ten shillings a week rise. Elsie has a brief fling with commercial traveller Walter Fletcher, but ditches him for the Detective Inspector. Her decree nisi from Arnold is granted. Billy Walker, Jack and Annie's son, is back from National Service and starts his first job as a mechanic at the Blue Bell Garage.

JUNE

Linda Cheveski goes into labour while visiting Dot Greenhalgh, Elsie's work-mate from Miami Modes, and the Street welcomes its first baby – Paul Cheveski weighs in at 7lb 2½oz. Ena takes a holiday in Bridlington to recover from her ankle injury. Ken Barlow closes the book on his affair with librarian Marion – their age difference is too great, he tells her.

At No. 5 Tom Hayes, a one-arm-bandit entrepreneur, moves in with his sister Esther. Mission-goer Emily Nugent closes her Mawdesley Street baby linen shop and amalgamates with Leonard Swindley's Rosamund Street haberdashery business.

JULY

Ken Barlow's exam results come through: BA 2nd Class Hons, English and History. Leo and Mario Bonarti open an Italian restaurant in Rosamund Street. Christine Hardman falls for handsome Mario's Latin charm.

AUGUST

Another exam success as Lucille Hewitt passes her 11-Plus. Florrie Lindley wins £500 on a new government scheme called Premium Bonds. Frank Barlow is promoted to supervisor at the GPO. Ken's pulse quickens as he meets Valerie Tatlock for the first time. Val has her own hairdresser's shop – Maison Valerie in Rosamund Street – and has moved into No. 1 with her Uncle Albert.

SEPTEMBER

Baby Paul Cheveski is christened, but tragedy mars the celebrations. Ida Barlow is horrifically killed beneath the wheels of a bus as she crosses the road. Tile Street Police Station investigates the accident.

OCTOBER

Rovers regulars go to Blackpool Illuminations. Glowering Ena is left behind by the bus and has to hitch a lift home on a lorry. On the coach trip home Harry Hewitt proposes to the Rovers Irish barmaid Concepta Riley. Their wedding reception is held at the Greenfield Hotel – Annie Walker is unequipped for catering – and the couple leave for a honeymoon at the Cresta Hotel, Port Erin.

Doreen Lostock takes over as barmaid at the Rovers. Ken Barlow goes into industry as assistant personnel officer at Amalgamated Steel.

Romance rears its head again for Elsie Tanner. An old Navy chum of Len Fairclough, Chief Petty Officer Bill Gregory, sweeps her off her feet and returns to his ship, leaving Elsie under the impression that he is single.

NOVEMBER

Business is bad for Leonard Swindley. Teetering on the brink of bankruptcy he is taken over by Spiros Papagopolous, and a new sign goes up: 'Gamma Garments'. Ken quits Amalgamated Steel after a row with his boss, and takes a teaching post at Bessie Street School.

Ena is caught again nursing a stout in the Rovers, and accused of intemperance by Leonard Swindley. She resigns in a huff from the Mission, and moves in with her friend Minnie Caldwell in Jubilee Terrace.

DECEMBER

The Cheveski's emigrate to a new home at 1207 Central Avenue, Montreal, where Ivan has found work as an engineer. Annie Walker enters the world of cuisine and provides the sandwiches for a farewell party at the Rovers. Elsie accompanies them to Ringway Airport by taxi for a tearful farewell. Ena, Martha and Minnie celebrate Christmas at the Rovers.

1962

JANUARY

Ken Barlow writes a controversial article for a left wing review, *Survival*, criticizing the working classes. The *Manchester Evening News* reprints it as 'Life In A Northern Back Street', and angry locals recognize themseves, thinly disguised. High-minded Ken accuses them of being unambitious and starved of culture. Len Fairclough calls it rubbish and punches him on the jaw in the Rovers.

FEBRUARY

Ena makes peace with Leonard Swindley and returns to life in the Vestry. Harry Hewitt exchanges his whippets for a greyhound called Lucky Lolita, which wins at 10–1. A coach trip eagerly sets out from the Rovers for the next White City race. Everyone bets £10 to win, but Lolita is not so lucky – they lose everything.

MARCH

Ena is found collapsed in the Vestry suffering from another slight stroke. Wayward Dennis Tanner quits his job as compere at the Orinoco night-club and leaves for London with his girlfriend, snake-dancer Eunice 'La Composita' Bond.

APRIL

Len Fairclough is sacked from J. Birtwistle and Sons when nosey Martha Longhurst reports him for doing 'foreigners'. He buys the yard behind Martha's Mawdesley Street home, and starts his own business.

MAY

Billy Walker announces his engagement to Finsbury beauty queen Phillipa Scopes, who is considered rather 'posh'. They part two weeks later by mutual agreement.

Ena Sharples fights a council proposal to rename the Street 'Florida Street', and writes a protest letter to Prince Philip. She receives a reply, but does not reveal its contents. Esther Hayes leaves the Street and moves into a flat in Moor Lane.

JUNE

Christine Hardman, jilted by local plumber Joe Makinson, has a nervous breakdown. Ken Barlow gently talks her down from the roof of the raincoat factory. Three weeks later she elopes with Colin Appleby.

Doreen Lostock is now working at Gamma Garments, and shares a flat over the corner shop with Sheila Birtles. Bill Gregory, home from the sea in uniform, resumes his relationship with Elsie Tanner. Len Fairclough warns him to tell Elsie he is married, but he says nothing.

JULY

Ken Barlow announces his engagement to Valerie Tatlock, and Bill Gregory's wife turns up at Elsie's. The affair breaks up and the chief petty officer goes home to mend his marriage. Minnie Caldwell's mother dies at their home in Jubilee Terrace. Ena affirms her belief in cremation. Jerry Booth, who lives with his mother in Viaduct Street, signs on as an apprentice for Len Fairclough. He served his time with Len's old boss, Joe White of Bessie Street.

The Telstar satellite is launched, and ever-watchful Martha Longhurst scans the night sky over Coronation Street. Annie Walker renews a holiday friendship when the dapper Mr Forsythe-Jones, whom she met in Babbacombe, drops in at the Rovers. Ken makes the supreme sacrifice and sells his scooter to pay for his wedding.

AUGUST

Ken and Valerie marry and leave for a honeymoon in London. Another birth in the Street: Harry and Concepta Hewitt have a son, Christopher, 7lb 3oz.

Minnie Caldwell moves into No. 5, Esther Hayes' old house, with Bobbie her tabby cat. Among her belongings is a china cat named Felix, which she won at Albert Croft Fair in 1921. The head is broken off, but Minnie can't bear to part with it.

SEPTEMBER

Leonard Swindley goes into politics as founder and chairman of the Property Owners and Small Traders Party. Ken Barlow treads new ground too – his first novel is rejected by a publisher. Elsie has been going out with artful bookie Dave Smith. Len, who strongly disapproves, assaults him and is bound over for twelve months.

OCTOBER

Baby Christopher Hewitt is kidnapped from outside Gamma Garments on Harry and Concepta's wedding anniversary. He was left outside in his pram by Lucille. Elsie tracks down the baby and recovers him from a stranger, Joan Akers. The drama earns *Coronation Street* the highest viewing figures in television history.

As Jack and Annie Walker celebrate their Silver Wedding, Colin Appleby is killed in a car crash. His devastated widow Christine returns to lodge with Elsie. Officious Albert Tatlock starts work as a lollipop man on the crossing near Bessie Street School.

NOVEMBER

Christine Appleby takes a job at Miami Modes and strikes up a relationshp with quiet, pipe-smoking widower Frank Barlow. Linda and Ivan Cheveski return home from Canada for Christmas, and Minnie Caldwell takes in a Liverpudlian lodger, Jed Stone. Leonard Swindley is hard on the election trail for the Property Owners and Small Traders Party. Result: bottom of the poll.

DECEMBER

Showtime in the Street: residents appear in *Lady Lawson Loses*, produced by Leonard Swindley at the Mission. As Christmas approaches Len Fairclough's wife Nellie leaves him for Harry Bailey, taking their son Stanley with her. Ken Barlow hands in his notice at Bessie Street School to embark on a full-time career as a writer, but withdraws after second thoughts.

The Street encounters its first racial problem. Black bus conductor Johnny Alexander accuses Len Fairclough of fare dodging. Len denies it and reports him to bus inspector Harry Hewitt. When the conductor is suspended, Len confesses that he had not paid his fare. Johnny refuses to take back his job on principle, despite a visit from Concepta begging him to reconsider. Jack and Annie decorate the Rovers for Christmas.

JANUARY

Jed Stone opens a market stall and takes on Sheila Birtles as his assistant. Her parents are shocked and order her to give it up. Gamma Garments supremo Spiros Papagopolous launches a cost-cutting drive and orders Leonard Swindley to sack Miss Nugent. Swindley pleads for her reinstatement and is told she can be kept on – if business improves.

FEBRUARY

Frank Barlow's affair with Christine Appleby causes gossip in the Street – and friction between Ken and Frank. As the Rovers buzzes about the romance, Albert tells everyone about his war service at the Somme in 1916.

MARCH

Christine and Frank announce their engagement. Rents in Coronation Street, Mawdesley Street and Viaduct Street are raised on Elsie Tanner's birthday. Late at night Jed Stone packs his bags and leaves the Street under a veil of secrecy. Ena Sharples' sister, Alice Raybould, dies aged eighty, leaving Ena £100. After paying for the funeral, Ena is £50 out of pocket.

APRIL

Christine tearfully breaks off her engagement to Frank – the age difference is just too great. Elsie is issued with an eviction order for refusing to pay the rent increase. When bailiffs put her furniture out on the pavement, Elsie agrees to pay – but only when they have carried her furniture inside again. On the same day Dennis Tanner returns home to take charge of the Lenny Phillips Theatrical Agency.

MAY

Frank Barlow resigns from the GPO and decides to go into business on his own. He opens a DIY shop at 152 Victoria Street. Romance blossoms as Elsie has her first date with Len Fairclough – they go to a dance at the Orinoco Club.

JUNE

The Street is invited round to the grand opening of Frank's new shop. Harry Hewitt agrees to move to Ireland and hands in his notice. On the last minute he changes his mind because he cannot bring himself to leave Lucille.

JULY

Leonard Swindley is transferred to Gamma Garments head office, and romeo Neil Crossley takes over as relief manager of the shop.

AUGUST

Lanky window cleaner Walter Potts is 'discovered' by Dennis Tanner, who becomes his manager and launches him on a pop-singing career as Brett Falcon. Albert Tatlock gets drunk with Alf Roberts on the Rovers darts team outing. A patrolling policeman finds Albert clinging to a lamp-post and, after a shouting match, charges them with assaulting an officer.

SEPTEMBER

Sheila Birtles attempts suicide with an Aspirin overdose in the wake of an affair with Gamma's relief manager Neil Crossley. Dennis Tanner, in a rare display of public-spiritedness, saves her by climbing a ladder to her flat window.

OCTOBER

Sheila leaves her flat above the Corner Shop and returns home, and her friend Doreen Lostock joins the WRAC. Ena returns home to find the Vestry vandalized. Walter Potts makes a shaky debut as Brett Falcon at Weatherfield Trades and Labour Club, but goes down well. Joiner Jerry Booth marries Myra Dickinson. There is almost a double celebration when Elsie Tanner's decree absolute comes through and Len proposes – but she turns him down.

NOVEMBER

Elsie, enjoying her freedom, launches into an affair with Orinoco Club owner Laurie Frazer. Ena collapses – the doctor diagnoses arterio-sclerosis – and she moves back in with Minnie Caldwell. Meanwhile, the Vestry vandal is caught – youngster Michael Butterworth who had been to juvenile court for stealing Ena's pension book.

DECEMBER

Walter Potts polishes up his stage act and becomes a successful pop singer. Dennis Tanner springs a 'This Is Your Life' on a shocked Annie Walker. The mystery guest is Mr Forsythe-Jones, who sings a duet with her.

JANUARY

Walter Potts leaves on his first European tour. Esther Hayes is promoted to the Civil Service Department of Statistics and moves from Moor Lane to Glasgow. Ken Barlow feels restive and applies for promotion at Bessie Street School.

FEBRUARY

A Bessie Street pupil is killed in a road accident and there are demands for a proper children's crossing. Ken is interviewed on TV about the issue, but handles it badly, killing his chances of promotion. To make things worse, Val has an affair with pacifist Dave Robbins, one of Ken's college friends, and leaves home. She returns later the same night and they make up.

MARCH

Ken is appointed Head of English at Granston Technical College. Len Fairclough challenges Jerry to a walking race for a £5 wager. The Street turns out at the recreation ground, the Red Rec, to watch. Jerry, a keep-fit fanatic, allows a panting Len to win and avoid losing face.

Laurie Frazer opens the Viaduct Sporting Club in the old raincoat factory. His wife turns up, bringing a swift end to his affair with Elsie. Leonard Swindley's troubles with Papagopolous bring on a nervous breakdown, and he leaves with his sister, Hilda Barrett. Florrie Lindley opens a sub-post office at the Corner Shop.

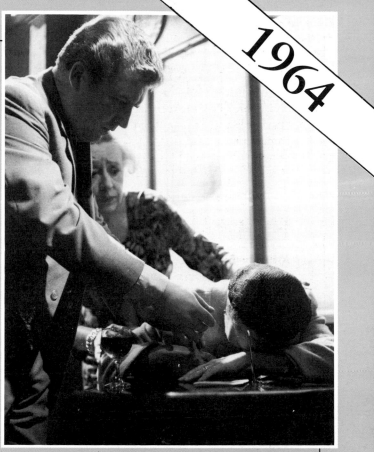

APRIL

At No. 13 Jerry's wife Myra is pregnant and they are in financial difficulty. Myra is poor at handling money, and the mortgage payments have fallen behind. Irma Ogden begins work at the Corner Shop.

MAY

Minnie Caldwell falls on the stairs at the Orinoco Club and injures herself. Martha advises her to claim compensation, and she sues Len Fairclough, who repaired the staircase. Jerry is sacked by Len, who can't afford to pay him, and the Booths move in with Myra's father in Viaduct Street.

   Frank Barlow wins £5,000 on the Premium Bonds and decides to sell his shop and move to Wilmslow. Tragedy hits his celebration party in the Rovers when Martha Longhurst collapses from a heart attack and dies.

JUNE

Charlie Moffitt, the Orinoco's stand-up comic, moves in to lodge with Minnie – along with a greyhound called Little Tich, three pigeons and two rabbits. Dennis Tanner takes up hairdressing and dyes Lucille's hair blonde. Lucille is already in trouble with her headmistress for having 'Brett Falcon Fan Club' tattooed on her wrist.

   The Ogdens, apparently a nice couple, appear in the Street: Stan puts down a £200 deposit on No. 13 and takes out a £575 mortgage. It is Leap Year and the ever-patient Miss Nugent decides to propose to Mr Swindley. Flustered, he refuses but relents and they become engaged.

JULY

The Street turns out for Miss Nugent's wedding. As Leonard Swindley waits uncomfortably at the altar, something is clearly wrong. Emily, agonizing over her choice of future husband, gets cold feet and jilts him. Elsie Tanner takes a job as a 'mature model' at the School of Design and wastes no time having an affair with art teacher David Graham.

AUGUST

David Graham, totally infatuated with her, threatens Elsie with a gun when she tries to break off the relationship. Dennis Tanner, with no thought for personal safety, intervenes and overpowers him. Lucille, Brett Falcon's biggest fan, wins a singing prize herself in a talent contest at the Sporting Club. Harry and Concepta Hewitt leave to take over a garage in Castle Blayney, Ireland.

Stan Ogden digs up an unexploded bomb in Albert Tatlock's back yard. The Street is evacuated to the Mission, and there is an air of wartime spirit as bomb disposal experts get to work.

SEPTEMBER

Irish comic Tickler Murphy, appearing at the Orinoco with Charlie Moffitt, moves in as Minnie's second lodger. The Ogdens have problems with their eldest son Trevor who steals some money and absconds to London. Valerie Barlow, in the meantime, announces she is pregnant.

OCTOBER

Tickler Murphy manages Stan Ogden as a wrestler and arranges a bout at the Viaduct Sporting Club with the formidable Ian Campbell. Stan is counted out after being thrown from the ring into Hilda's lap.

Ena breaks the news to Len that she has had a visit from Harry Bailey, who called to tell her that Len's ex-wife Nellie is dead. Len and Elsie embark on a trial daytime marriage under the surveillance of Minnie Caldwell.

NOVEMBER

Trouble at the Rovers: Stan secretly stops the pub clock at a hot-pot supper, to gain more drinking time, and Jack Walker is charged with selling drinks after-hours. Jack's problems are only beginning. He has been quietly paying Billy's rent. Annie finds the cheque book stubs, addressed to the landlady Mrs Nicholls. Suspecting him of infidelity, she walks out. Len Fairclough decides that his son Stanley should stay with Harry Bailey.

DECEMBER

Billy Walker returns to sort out the trouble between Annie and Jack. Ena traces Annie to the Egremont Hotel and brings her back. Wealthy butcher Willy Piggott offers Ken Barlow a £100 bribe to help his son through his exams. Ken indignantly refuses and reports him to the police. Footballer David Barlow limps home with a leg injury and embarks on an affair with Irma Ogden. He hears he has been suspended from football on bribery charges.

Stan Ogden goes into partnership with Albert Tatlock and Charlie Moffitt in a waste paper business. Emily Nugent stages *Cinderella* at the Mission and plays Dandini.

JANUARY

Ena is left No. 11 in a will. She studies the Rent Act and to Elsie's anger raises the rent. When Elsie objects, she is given notice to quit. The Mission, which has been threatened with demolition, is reprieved, and Ena sells the deeds to No. 11 to local landlord Edward Wormold for £350.

Leonard Swindley is promoted to Gamma Garments' head office. Jerry Booth returns to the street to work for Len after leaving his wife Myra and lodges with Florrie Lindley.

FEBRUARY

Stan's waste paper enterprise collapses through lack of customers. Hilda winds it up and he starts as a milk roundsman. Piggott is remanded on £100 bail for bribery. Ena lends Charlie Moffitt £50 to set up as an insurance agent. Florrie Lindley's engineer husband Norman returns and immediately has a brief fling with Elsie.

MARCH

Emily Nugent takes on Elsie as a sales assistant at Gamma Garments. Emily buys a Morris Minor and Mr Swindley returns to give her driving lessons. She is arrested and charged with driving the wrong way up a one-way street. Swindley's licence is found to have expired and they end up in the dock together. He is fined £25, Miss Nugent £5.

APRIL

Val Barlow gives birth to twins – Susan and Peter. David Barlow is cleared on the soccer bribery charges, but decides to quit league football. Willy Piggott is less fortunate – he is fined £150 for the exam bribery attempt.

Piggott has financed a building development in Blackburn, on which Len loses £1,000. Jerry takes over the job and walks out on Len.

MAY

A relieved Miss Nugent passes her driving test. Norman and Florrie Lindley emigrate to Canada, and Lionel Petty takes over the Corner Shop. David Barlow signs a two-year contract as player-coach for Weatherfield Athletic. Ena's great-nephew arrives on holiday from Nebraska.

JUNE

Lionel Petty's daughter Sandra serves in the Corner Shop and falls for her first customer, Dennis Tanner. David Barlow and Irma Ogden become engaged on a day trip to the Blue John Mines at Speedwell. Ena accepts an invitation to visit Nebraska and flies out from Ringway.

JULY

Elsie is sacked by Miss Nugent in a Gamma staff economy drive, and takes a job at the local laundrette, the Laundryer. Clara Midgeley appears in the Street as Ena's relief help at the Mission. Stan Ogden and Charlie Moffitt brew their own beer at Minnie's. As Miss Nugent and Minnie get quietly drunk, the bottles explode.

AUGUST

Jerry Booth's building venture collapses and he returns cap in hand to Len, who offers him a partnership. Dennis Tanner and Sandra Petty look as though they are falling in love.

Lucille Hewitt's exam results come through – four O-levels, including science and geography. Her old home, No. 7, which has been empty since the Hewitts left, collapses and has to be demolished by Len and Jerry.

SEPTEMBER

Ena returns from holiday in Nebraska. Elsie, visiting the Fox and Hounds pub, in Cheshire, is picked up by tweedy Robert Maxwell. On the way home he collapses and dies behind the wheel of his Jaguar. Elsie flees in panic and catches a bus home. An inquest returns a verdict of death from natural causes, but a bitter Mrs Maxwell blames Elsie.

OCTOBER

Jerry moves in to lodge with Len. Lucille quits her job at Mitchell's Mail Order to work in the research and development department at Marshall's Cotton Mill. The Street's lady residents take part in a charity mannequin parade at the Mission, organized by Miss Nugent.

NOVEMBER

Annie Walker's dreams are fulfilled when she is made chairman of the Lady Victuallers, and presented with a chain of office. Dennis Tanner has a telephone installed at No. 11, and Elsie has a whirlwind affair with telephone engineer Jim Mount.

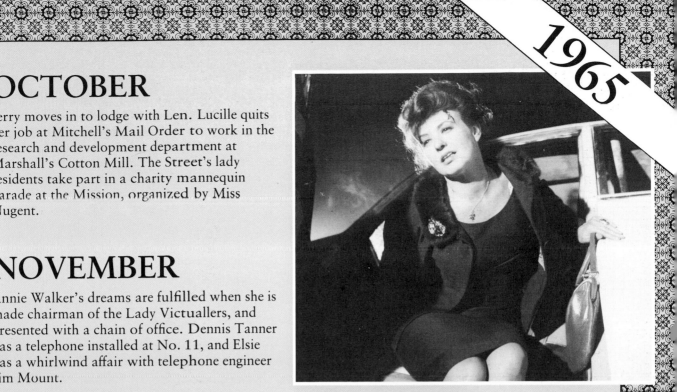

DECEMBER

David Barlow and Irma Ogden slip away for a secret Register Office wedding, but the news is leaked by a talkative taxi-driver. The Street turn up to surprise them at a reception at the Greenvale Hotel.

Lucille, under age, is caught serving behind the bar of the Rovers by Jack Turner. Jerry Booth beats up Turner when he hears that Jack Walker is being blackmailed over the incident. David Barlow receives a leg injury in a charity soccer match, and learns that he will never play again. The club ends his contract and gives him £300 compensation.

JANUARY

Ken Barlow has an affair with *Weatherfield Gazette* reporter Jackie Marsh, who covered David's accident. Val, meanwhile, is given a piano and has lessons from Ena. After strong disagreements, David and Irma Barlow decide to buy the Corner Shop from Lionel Petty. An ecstatic Stan Ogden celebrates eight draws on the football coupon – only to find that Hilda has incorrectly filled it in.

Jed Stone returns and resumes life at Minnie's. Emily Nugent has an offer from holiday friend St John Hunter to manage a souvenir shop in Majorca.

FEBRUARY

Albert Tatlock becomes friendly with Clara Midgeley and they visit Cleveleys together. After a farewell party Miss Nugent leaves ostensibly for Majorca, but conscience beckons. At the last minute she secretly goes to Harrogate to nurse her father, who is recovering from a stroke. Nasty Ray Langton appears in the Street and plunges into an affair with Lucille. He steals £5 from the Barlows when they baby-sit together.

MARCH

Clara Midgeley proposes to Albert, who decides she is too pushy and turns her down. Elsie disconnects her feelings for telephone engineer Jim Mount when she finds he has no serious intentions of marriage. Jed Stone teams up with Dennis Tanner to run boarding kennels under the Viaduct.

1966

APRIL

Valerie tackles Ken about his affair with Jackie Marsh, but he swears it was platonic. Len sacks light-fingered Ray Langton for stealing a bottle of whiskey from the Rovers, and deducts the cost, along with the Barlow's £5, from his wages. Ray leaves the Street.

Ena Sharples, who has given her life savings to her daughter Vera, is caught shop-lifting in the Pick-a-Snip supermarket and fined £2. To add to her problems the Mission is scheduled for demolition. Social worker Ruth Winter tries to rehouse her, but Ena stubbornly refuses to co-operate.

MAY

Despite the disapproval of Annie Walker and David Barlow, Lucille and Irma both take £15 a week jobs at the newly-opened Elliston's Raincoat Factory. Bet Lynch makes her first appearance in the Street as a rag-trade employee, and Annie considers her 'rather common'.

Stan buys an ice-cream van but his rivals, the Bonarti's take all his business. Stan has to give up and sell off his surplus stock. Minnie is depressed because her cat Bobbie has the flu. Jed Stone takes her to the Orinoco Club to watch Randolph Sutton, to cheer her up.

JUNE

Stan Ogden takes up the offer of an ice-cream round for the Bonarti's. Hilda suspects Stan of having an affair with Mrs Rose Bonarti and reports him for trading without a licence. Sheila Birtles returns from Rawtenstall, to lodge with Elsie and take a job at the raincoat factory. Jerry Booth and Sheila resume their affair.

AUGUST

Jerry seeks a divorce from Myra, and runs into opposition from her father, George Dickinson. A glowing Annie is nominated by Colonel and Mrs Arkinstall as a candidate for the Federation of Women's Associations in the local election.

Annie is horrified when Jack insults the Colonel at a British Legion reunion, but all is not lost – Mrs Arkinstall diplomatically praises Jack's 'unyielding qualities'.

SEPTEMBER

Election Day. Len opposes Annie as Independent candidate. They tie, but after a recount the result is the same. Len wins on the toss of a coin. At the Corner Shop, David and Irma are visited by a health inspector after the potted meat for the election party causes food poisoning.

Hilda and Stan join David and Irma for a weekend away from it all in Wales. Their caravan is marooned by cattle, and an angry farmer threatens them with legal action. Jed Stone is arrested at Minnie's birthday party for receiving stolen blankets, and sentenced to eighteen months.

JULY

Dennis Tanner returns to the Street £94 in debt from a gaming fiddle that backfired. Bookie Dave Smith makes Elsie an offer – he will pay the debt in return for 'favours'. Elsie refuses and Len gives Dennis a job to help him out. Ken Barlow holds an evening of cultural films at the Mission, but the distributors send nudist movies by mistake.

OCTOBER

Linda and Ivan Cheveski return from Canada. Elsie, sacked from the Laundryer for taking time off, receives anonymous phone calls. They are traced to widow Mrs Robert Maxwell, who has become mentally disturbed.

Jed Stone, in Walton Jail, asks Minnie to auction his belongings. Neighbours conspire to offer more than they are worth. Annie Walker bids for a two shilling cameo brooch and discovers it is worth £15.

NOVEMBER

Young Paul Cheveski goes missing and is pulled from the canal by an unknown rescuer. Elsie rounds on Len, who blocked council proposals to fence the canal for financial reasons. Paul's father Ivan reads a newspaper report, which also blames Len, and after two pints, punches him. Later, in the Rovers, they make it up.

DECEMBER

Stan Ogden faces Christmas on the dole after being made redundant from his milk round. Elsie returns to Miami Modes as supervisor. Former Gamma relief manager Neil Crossley leaves the Street arm-in-arm with Sheila Birtles – they plan to marry.

Ena's daughter Vera stays with her because she cannot cope at home. Ena accuses her of malingering, unaware that she is dying of a brain tumor. Val and Ken Barlow throw a Street fancy dress party in the Mission for Christmas. Annie Walker surprises no one by going as Queen Elizabeth I.

JANUARY

Stan Ogden's dole is stopped when he turns down work, and he has to take a job as a coal heaver. Dennis Tanner resigns from the yard after setting fire to Len's kitchen with a blow-lamp while decorating. He takes up an offer from Miss Nugent at Gamma Garments, and persudes Lucille to join him.

Imposter Percy Bridge poses as Paul Cheveski's canal rescuer and is rewarded by Elsie. Bookie Dave Smith exposes him by producing Paul's cap, proving that it was he who rescued him. Ena's daughter Vera dies of a brain tumor.

FEBRUARY

Stan Ogden fills Dennis' old job at Len's yard and makes an impressive start by spraining his back and having the first week off sick. The new-look Gamma Garments opens: Miss Nugent invites Councillor Fairclough to cut the tape, but Dennis has booked a beauty queen without telling her.

Albert Tatlock is knocked unconscious during a raid on Dave Smith's shop, while placing a bet for Minnie. Ena launches a petition to have it closed down. Ken Barlow is protesting too – he joins a banned student demonstration against the Vietnam War.

MARCH

Ken is arrested at the demonstration and fined £5. On grounds of conscience he opts for seven days' jail instead. Emily Nugent timidly takes the plunge and has swimming lessons from Jerry Booth.

Annie Walker rows with Jack over his answers to money questions in a light-hearted truth game in the Rovers. Jack storms out and spends the night with Albert Tatlock. Frosty Annie is convinced he slept with Elsie Tanner, but Ena steps in and reconciles them.

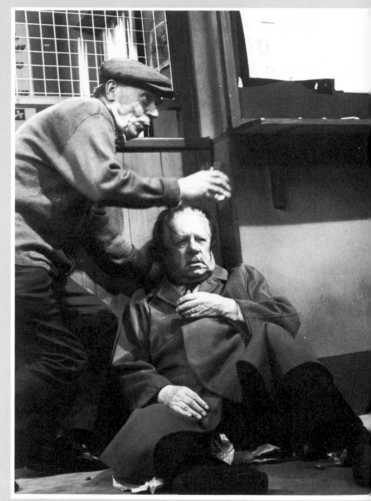

APRIL

Minnie Caldwell's £50 insurance policy matures after thirty years, but she immediately loses £20 to a con-man masquerading as a plumber. Ken Barlow turns down a council nomination for the Ratepayers' Party and his brother David becomes coach to Weatherfield Hotspurs – an all-ladies soccer team.

The Yanks are coming: Elsie gets a phone call from American wartime friend, Master Sergeant Steve Tanner, who has been posted to Burtonwood. Meanwhile, Gregg Flint, who served at the base during the war, returns with a pal named Gerry Strauss, and resumes his friendship with Dot Greenhalgh.

MAY

Lucille celebrates her eighteenth birthday. Elsie and Steve Tanner rekindle their twenty-year-old flame. Len Fairclough is returned unopposed in the local elections.

Then disaster: a goods train ploughs through the Viaduct parapet and plunges into the Street. Ena Sharples is buried under the wreckage and dug out by David Barlow. A local girl, Sonia Peters, is killed. Her boyfriend, Jimmy Conway, is dragged from the rubble by rescuer Jerry Booth. Ena, still suffering from bruises and shock, discharges herself from Weatherfield Hospital and turns up at the Rovers.

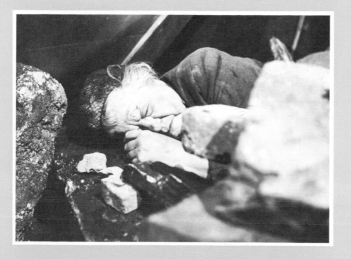

JUNE

GI Steve Tanner is beaten up by Dot Greenhalgh's husband, who mistakes him for Gregg Flint. Steve takes Elsie for a night out to the romantic Roebuck Inn, Cheshire, and proposes to her. Elsie accepts.

Dennis Tanner's blonde Swedish girlfriend Inga Olsen returns home, and he takes a bar job in Amsterdam to be nearer to her. Ena enters Coronation Street for the 'Best Kept Street' Competition. Less than two weeks later squatters Betty Lawson, and her sons Clifford and Ronnic, take over No. 3.

JULY

Ken Barlow rows with Val about her sympathetic attitude to the squatters, and demands that Len has them evicted. Lucille sends for cosmetics brochures in Annie's name, but the joke backfires – Annie wins a weekend in Paris with a film star as Cuty Beauty's millionth customer.

A £300 deficiency is discovered in Fairclough and Booth's accounts. Len has been secretly investing in council property without telling Jerry. Dennis Tanner returns with Inga's sister Karen, his new girlfriend. He applies to make her his au pair, and signs the letter Steve Tanner.

AUGUST

Dennis, visited by a consular official, borrows Val's twins and persuades Lucille to masquerade as his wife. The official tumbles the ruse and orders Karen into proper employment.

Hilda is seen boarding a Liverpool-bound bus in her house-slippers. Police find her wandering disturbed near the Pier Head. Her purse contains £40 which Stan held as treasurer of the Rovers Outing Fund. The money is refunded but Stan loses it to Albert Tatlock in a card game. Steve Tanner and Len challenge Albert to pitch-and-toss to get the money back, but he wins again. Albert finally hands it over to teach Stan a lesson. Emily organizes a coach trip to Tatton Park.

SEPTEMBER

Steve and Elsie marry at St Stephen's Methodist Church, Warrington, near the air base, and leave for a honeymoon in Lisbon. Tragedy mars the occasion as Harry Hewitt, back from Ireland for the wedding, is crushed to death when a jack collapses under Len's van. Concepta arrives to identify the body. With Elsie away, Dennis Tanner takes in theatrical lodgers – a girls' pipe band, followed by two acrobats, the Pinelli Brothers, and their mother Mrs Cooke.

OCTOBER

Len Fairclough's son, Stanley, comes to stay
with him, but there is friction between them.
Stanley sets fire to the yard, to get back at his
father, and is overcome by the flames. Len
attempts to drag him free, but collapses. Stan
Ogden rescues them both, and Stanley goes
back to his stepfather Harry Bailey. Emily
Nugent visits a marriage bureau and makes a
date with farmer Frank Starkey. She visits his
farm, but finds she is terrified of cows, and the
liaison ends.

NOVEMBER

Elsie Tanner's overpowering American
mother-in-law Emmeline arrives to inspect
Elsie. She clearly disapproves and there is a
first-class row. Ena Sharples turns down an
offer to move to St Annes and become
housekeeper for her late husband's wealthy
friend Henry Foster.

Emily tries the marriage bureau again and
becomes engaged to private hotelier Douglas
Preston, who is dominated by his sister Amy.
Emily regretfully breaks it off when she realizes
that his only motive is escape.

DECEMBER

Annie Walker visits a football match to
broaden her outlook. Provoked by hooligans,
she hurls a rattle at them and smashes a
window. A stunned Annie is arrested and a
toilet roll, planted by a supporter, is found in
her bag. The charge is dropped when Len
intercedes.

Irma, who has had a miscarriage, is turned
down for adoption. She and David take a
foster child, Jill Morris, for Christmas. Elsie
and Steve leave Ringway on a flight to Boston.
Dennis wastes no time in turning No. 11 into a
hippy commune. Albert Tatlock organizes a
Christmas tug of war against the Flying Horse.
The Rovers lose and Albert grudgingly awards
the winners a pint of beer each.

JANUARY

Ena is evicted from the Mission. Bulldozers move in to demolish the home she has lived in for thirty years, along with the raincoat factory. Irma Barlow arranges a date between lonely Emily and macho Hungarian building worker Miklos Zadic.

Hilda feels lonely and strikes up a friendship with park gardener George Greenwood. He buys Hilda a budgie which she keeps in his hut. When Stan finds out, they part – but George keeps the budgie. Lucille joins the hippies at No. 11, and Dennis finds a new girlfriend, Cockney Jenny Sutton. They start as waiter and receptionist at Weatherfield Social Club.

FEBRUARY

Ena decides to move to St Annes after all. Elsie returns alone from America with the news that Steve has been posted to Panama. Albert's house is ransacked and his prized coin collection stolen. He accuses Miklos Zadic, but police catch the real thief. Annie Walker is kidnapped by rag students and held for £5 ransom. There are no takers, and she stonily has to pay for her own release.

MARCH

Elsie Tanner announces that she has left Steve. Their marriage, she says, was a twenty-year-old dream. Dennis returns from London with girlfriend Jenny, and tells Elsie they are married and can share the same bed. Under close interrogation he confesses that he was kidding. Dennis becomes a rep for Crowning Glory Hair Requisites.

Irma Ogden is pregnant and plans to emigrate to Australia with David. They put the shop up for sale, but encounter little interest because of a slum clearance programme.

APRIL

Maggie and Les Clegg buy the Corner Shop. Outgoing Maggie is interested in herbalism and stocks natural remedies, Les has a drink problem. Their son Gordon, a trainee accountant, joins them.

Miklos takes a job in Newcastle and Emily leaves with him. Three weeks later she returns alone, tight-lipped, and moves into the Rovers as a paying guest. Len advertizes for a plumber, and Jerry hires Ray Langton in his absence. Irma and David leave for Australia.

MAY

Len is furious, and sparks fly when he meets Ray. Jerry has to break up a fight between them. Finally Len grudgingly agrees to take him on. An entire building site downs tools when Stan Ogden walks onto the job, and he quits to work in Fairclough and Booth's yard.

Elsie proudly refuses to touch any of Steve's weekly allowance and works at a department store, distributing samples of fish paste on crackers. Dennis borrows £100 from a money lender at 48 per cent interest to marry Jenny. On his wedding night his boss at Crowning Glory orders him immediately to Bristol, leaving Jenny alone in the double bed.

JUNE

Ken Barlow is allocated a maisonette and sells his Mini to buy furniture. Len buys No. 9 for £1,000, Ena returns and moves into a maisonette, and a young couple – Audrey Bright and Dickie Fleming – buy No. 3 for £400.

Les Clegg is admitted to a mental hospital suffering from alcoholism, and Ena helps out in the Corner Shop. Stan Ogden gives Elsie a driving lesson, but they run out of petrol and have to spend the night on the moors. Suspicious Hilda accuses Elsie of having designs on Stan.

131

JULY

Jack Walker meets Ena's new neighbour, his childhood sweetheart Effie Spicer. Jealous Annie warns her off when she joins Jack's bowling club and calls him by his pet name, 'Jonty'. Ray Langton becomes Elsie's lodger and wastes no time making advances. Elsie, indignant, throws him out and Len takes him in at No. 9.

Audrey Bright, who is still at school, elopes to Gretna Green to marry Dickie Fleming. Ena, annoyed that Minnie has forsaken her for Effie Spicer, joins forces with Annie to get rid of her.

AUGUST

Escaped convict Frank Riley holds Val Barlow prisoner in her maisonette while Ken is attending drama class. She manages to tap a message on the central heating pipes, and Ena raises the alarm. Ken cannot believe that Val was not raped.

Ena is reported for excessive harmonium practice and reluctantly agrees to restrict her playing hours. Audrey Fleming takes a job as an £8 a week petrol pump attendant. Dave Smith buys the old Gamma shop, which closed when Papagopolous went bankrupt, and opens a flower shop called the Posy Bowl. Elsie is appointed manageress.

SEPTEMBER

Steve Tanner persuades two army buddies, Gary Strauss and Joe Donelli, to talk Elsie into meeting him again. Elsie agrees and returns distressed when he asks her to fly to America. Soon afterwards, Steve is found dead at the foot of the stairs in his flat. Gregg Flint, whom Steve was blackmailing over an affair with Dot Greenhalgh, is unable to offer an alibi.

Miss Nugent agrees to mind Tommy Deakin's donkey, Dolores, while he is away. Annie emphatically bans it from the Rovers, but Maggie Clegg offers to keep it behind the shop. So many customers complain of the smell that Annie is forced to relent and stable it in the pub yard. Audrey Fleming wins £50 as 'Miss Petrol Pump' at the Blue Bell garage.

OCTOBER

As detectives investigate Steve Tanner's death, the finger of suspicion falls on the Street. Len Fairclough, seen at Steve's flat, is questioned by police about his injured hand. Donelli and Strauss have alibis. Gregg Flint reveals he was with a woman in Altrincham. Stan Ogden, after some hesitation, confesses he was in the Flying Horse with Mrs Regan from 19 Inkerman Street.

Len disappears on an extended binge and a developer cancels his building contract. Elsie, after asking Ken Barlow's advice, takes up an invitation to go on holiday with bookie Dave Smith.

NOVEMBER

Gordon Clegg proposes to Lucille, but Maggie forbids him to marry. Len returns to find his firm's funds exhausted, and Ray Langton turns down his offer of a partnership.

Ken Barlow takes up the trumpet again and plays at the Ogden's wedding anniversary. Minnie's cat Bobbie is stuck on the top of the Viaduct. Stan climbs up with difficulty and despite getting scratched, rescues him. It turns out to be a different cat.

DECEMBER

Lucille and Gordon, determined to marry, run away to Gretna, but have second thoughts in the buffet at Preston station and return home sheepishly. Albert, who has been away attending to his duties as curator of his regimental museum at Bury, takes up residence at No. 1 again. Rovers regulars stage *Aladdin*, produced by Emily Nugent and the vicar, the Rev Reginald James.

Eye-catching Marjorie Griffin turns up from Len's past on his doorstep and promptly moves in with him. Bobbie is still missing, so Minnie decides to keep the Viaduct stray and call him Sunny Jim, after Jed Stone.

JANUARY

Stan Ogden dabbles in antiques but gives it up to launch Hilda as a full-time clairvoyant. Minnie Caldwell, laying secret bets at Dave Smith's shop, shows signs of becoming a compulsive gambler. Billy Walker returns from London with a Chinese girlfriend, Jasmine Chong, much to Annie's disapproval.

Len tries to ditch old flame Marjorie, who has left her husband, by proposing to her. He is flabbergasted when she accepts, and her husband Basil calls with her clothes and her pet monkey Marlon. Desperate Len borrows two local lads, aged two and twelve, and passes them off as his sons. Majorie finally goes back to Basil.

FEBRUARY

Janice Langton, Ray's deliquent sister, turns up at No. 9. Len likes her and lets her stay – she has learned to cook at approved school. Val Barlow consults Madame Hilda for a tea cup reading and is told she is going to have a baby.

Minnie disappears from home, leaving a note: 'Look after Sunny Jim.' She owes Dave Smith £10 in gambling debts, and is taken to hospital as an 'unknown person found collapsed'. Janice leaves briskly after stealing Dave Smith's Jag, and Ena threatens to tell the Inland Revenue about the car unless he wipes clean Minnie's debt.

MARCH

Gordon and Lucille fix a wedding date. Lucille buys the dress and makes the arrangements, but a worried Gordon backs out on the last minute. They part as friends. Minnie, who is being treated in hospital for exposure, pleads with nurses to keep her whereabouts secret from the formidable Ena.

Alice Pickens moves in as Albert's lodger and hints to Hilda that she plans to marry him. Emily has a date with the vicar, but decides he is too naive: he believes that the Street's materialistic values outweigh its spiritual ones.

134

APRIL

Albert has had enough and decides to evict Alice, along with her mynah bird Kitchener. He stacks her belongings on the pavement, and she moves in with Minnie. Dave Smith's wife Lillian hires a private eye to tail Elsie. When divorce proceedings threaten a third of his income, he capitulates and agrees to pay her a weekly allowance.

Stan and Hilda have a day out in Derbyshire, but miss the train home and have to hitch a ride on a milk float. Ena organizes a sit-in against plans to demolish the Pensioners' Club-room to make way for a car park. She is arrested by PC Wilcox, but allowed off with a caution. Ray Langton begins an affair with newly-wed Audrey Fleming.

MAY

Alice Pickins abandons her quest for Albert and leaves to look after her eighty-year-old uncle in West Hartlepool. Dickie Fleming quits his job to work in an amusement arcade where he is having an affair with a slot-machine cashier.

Annie, striving to bring sophistication to the Street, decorates the Rovers with clogs and miners' lamps and collects signatures for the 'Perfect Landlady' competition. She wins a trip to Majorca for two, and invites Ena to join her. Dickie loses his job at the arcade.

JUNE

Maggie Clegg's sister, Betty Turpin, arrives in the Street with her husband Cyril, a police sergeant, and takes a job at the Rovers. Ena returns from Majorca alone – Annie telegrams Jack to say she is returning with a gentleman friend.

Len is in financial trouble, and Elsie slips Jack Walker £300 to lend him in his name. Len then reveals he wants the money to get married. He introduces Elsie to town hall clerk Janet Reid, who confides that she does not love Len, but hasn't the heart to tell him. When she plucks up courage, Len blames Elsie and slaps her across the face. Elsie, angry and upset, leaves the Street in a taxi, shouting that she is going for ever.

JULY

Annie returns with brewery representative Douglas Cresswell, and an offer. She and Jack have been asked to manage a pub in Majorca. They accept, but the brewery turns them down, because of Jack's age. Len makes up with Elsie and sells his van to repay the £300.

Stan Ogden borrows £50 to buy fifty suit lengths from 'Billy Oilcloth' on the market. He plans to sell them for £10 each but Hilda, mistakenly believing they are stolen, sells them for £1 each when Stan is out. Unstoppable Alice Pickens arrives at Albert's regimental museum while he is giving a conducted tour. He falls off the platform in shock, breaking his arm and cracking two ribs. The doctor gives him an ultimatum: either Alice moves in to nurse him, or he goes to hospital.

AUGUST

Albert, on advice from Val and Ken, proposes to Alice Pickens. They book a honeymoon suite in Morecambe, and Albert gets drunk on his stag night. He is found sitting beneath a lamp-post singing: *'If I Ruled the World'*.

Ray Langton, now working for himself, takes on Audrey Fleming as his clerk. Annie, who takes a dislike to Betty Turpin, asks Jack to get rid of her, but relents because they are short-handed.

SEPTEMBER

Albert's wedding is doomed – the vicar's car breaks down and he fails to turn up for the service. They call it off and Alice, rather than waste the tickets, goes to Morecambe alone for a holiday.

Stan Ogden becomes an Arthur Dooley-style sculptor. Gallery owner Bernard Fleming enthusiastically sponsors an exhibition of the new primitive's work, but dustmen take the exhibits thinking they are junk. Rovers regulars are challenged to a football match by the Flying Horse.

OCTOBER

Hilda scores – for the Flying Horse. The match is a draw, but the Rovers win the toss, and a barrel of beer from Annie. Squatters move into the empty flat next to Ken and Val. Ken supports them because his old college chum Dave Robbins is their spokesman, but Val wants them out. Elsie, now back at Miami Modes, collects a parcel for Dot Greenhalgh. It contains stolen dresses and she is charged with shop-lifting.

Stan Ogden and Betty Turpin secretly sign up with a slimming club – Fatties Anonymous. Hilda tails him, convinced he is meeting the woman from Inkerman Street. She eavesdrops on the slimming session, and glows proudly to hear Stan make a public testimonial that he wants to make himself more attractive to his wife. The Rovers take a coach trip to Windermere on a bus which has faulty steering. The hire company frantically alerts the police, but they are unable to trace them. The coach runs off a moorland road, injuring all the passengers, who are ferried to hospital.

NOVEMBER

Ena, who escaped with bruises, keeps an all-night vigil at the bedside of unconscious Minnie Caldwell. Maggie Clegg has a fractured pelvis, and Albert has broken his arm – in the same place as before. Ray Langton is paralysed from the waist down, and transferred to an orthopaedic hospital. Annie Walker organizes a collection for the widow of the coach driver. Elsie appears in court for shop-lifting.

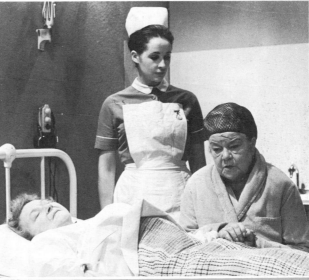

DECEMBER

Alan Howard appears in the Street and offers Val Barlow the job of manageress at a hairdressing salon he is opening at the Posy Bowl. Ken, who has an old-fashioned view about wives working, is against it. Jack and Albert get drunk at a regimental reunion.

Ray Langton leaves hospital in a wheelchair and stays with Audrey and Dickie. Betty Turpin is sacked from the Rovers after more friction with Annie. The Street hold a Christmas Talent Night. Ken plays his trumpet, Minnie recites *The Owl And The Pussycat*, Albert performs a monologue and Irma Barlow, who has returned for the holiday, impersonates Hilda Baker.

JANUARY

Betty, now working at the Flying Horse, returns to the Rovers after wringing a grudging apology from Annie. Elsie and Alan Howard start a 'no-strings' relationship. Paralysed Ray becomes engaged to Elsie's niece, Sandra Butler. He makes up his differences with Len and agrees to a partnership. Maggie Clegg and her husband Les seek a divorce. Len has a brief affair with Maggie, but leaves her for the barmaid at the Flying Horse.

FEBRUARY

Bill Gregory, now retired from the sea, turns up again. He is buying a business in Portugal and proposes to Elsie, who turns him down. Emily Nugent accepts a partnership with Ernest Bishop in his photographic business. Albert, Minnie and Ena visit the New Mission in Victoria Street, and Ena puts the harmonium through its paces.

MARCH

Ray Langton recovers the use of his legs and is soon caught in a passionate embrace with Audrey Fleming. Elsie falls in love with Alan Howard. Stan Ogden sells a song written by Ena, passing it off as his own. Ena rumbles him and writes another which, unknown to Stan, is *Onward Christian Soldiers*.

Annie, like Lysistrata, persuades the girls to withdraw all favours until the men sign a petition protesting against the football bus stopping in Coronation Street. Ken tries to buy Alan Howard's hairdressing salon for Val, but is out-bid by Dave Smith.

APRIL

Hilda receives news that David Barlow, and her grandson Darren, have been killed in an Australian car crash. Dave Smith lends her £600 to fly out and bring Irma home. Audrey Fleming tells Ray she loves him, and he admits he feels the same about her.

MAY

Weatherfield Gazette readers raise £600 for Hilda's air fare but, instead of repaying Dave Smith, Stan uses the money to buy Irma a partnership in the Corner Shop. Dickie and Audrey patch up their marriage and leave the Street for Huddersfield.

Sandra Butler accuses Ray of two-timing and becomes the first girl to give him the brush-off. Sergeant Cyril Turpin arrives home to find that Betty has been terrorized by ex-prisoner Keith Lucas. He furiously confronts Lucas with an iron bar, and only Len's intervention prevents him from killing Lucas.

JUNE

Len's evidence helps clear Cyril at the Police Disciplinary Enquiry. Cyril is allowed to retire from the force with a full pension, and takes a clerical job. He and Betty move to a house of their own. Jack Walker dies suddenly while visiting his daughter Joan, and is buried near her home in Derby.

JULY

Widowed Irma Barlow, under great nervous strain, steals a baby. Bet Lynch and Emily Nugent quietly return it before the alarm is raised. Minnie rekindles her friendship with an old school flame, Handel Gartside, who has returned from Quebec. Elsie and Alan Howard marry quietly at Weatherfield Register Office and, after informal drinks at the Rovers, leave for a honeymoon in Paris.

AUGUST

Alan Howard is insolvent, but his creditors give him a chance to repay his debts without official bankruptcy. Billy Walker returns to the Rovers after his father's death. He opens a garage in Canal Street and offers Alan a mechanic's job.

Ena discovers Tony Parsons, an organ-playing boy prodigy. By persuading his parents, and terrorizing the selection board, she helps him win a place at music college.

SEPTEMBER

Rag-and-bone man Tommy Deakin kennels his greyhound, Duke, at the Ogdens, leaving a special diet of port and steak. Hilda drinks the port, eats the steak and feeds the dog on scraps. Everyone in the Street bets on it, but it refuses to race.

New moves: Elsie starts as a rep for Charm Cosmetics, Lucille joins the Salvation Army as a helper and Annie is made licensee of the Rovers. Bet Lynch starts a relationship with ex-Borstal boy Frank Bradley, and reveals that she has an illegitimte son. Maggie and Irma take a holiday, recklessly leaving Hilda in charge of the shop. She stocks up with expensive delicatessen food which nobody wants.

OCTOBER

Irma returns to a loss of £7.2s.9d, and finds that half her customers have abandoned her. Lucille champions local gypsies and clashes with Ray who wants them evicted. Ken Barlow is awarded a grant to study technical education methods in New York. Minnie makes Ena jealous by cooking Handel Gartside's meals. Albert changes his hairdresser – and regrets it.

NOVEMBER

Albert discovers that Handel was a World War I conscientious objector, and sends him a white feather. Handel disapproves when Billy Walker moves in with Minnie while the Rovers is redecorated.

Irma becomes friendly with US Army Sergeant Joe Donnelli, who says he has been demobbed. Gregg Flint and Gary Strauss arrive and claim he is a deserter. Cornered, he takes Irma hostage, confessing to her that he killed Steve Tanner. Miss Nugent quits her barmaid's job at the Rovers because of her Mission convictions.

DECEMBER

Irma manages to escape. Donnelli takes refuge in Minnie's, holding her at gunpoint. Stan Ogden bravely talks him into releasing her, and Donnelli shoots himself. The Street's Christmas party is cancelled because of the tragedy.

Bet Lynch leaves the laundrette to work as a barmaid at the Rovers. Miss Nugent writes to Ken in America telling him that Val is having an affair – she is, in fact innocently taking driving lessons from Ray Langton.

JANUARY

Ken, back from New York, accepts a teaching post at the Randal Hart School, Montego Bay. He is shattered when, on the night of the farewell party, Val is electrocuted by a faulty hair-dryer plug and killed.

An outraged Annie has been accused by the Health Department of watering the Rovers gin. Stan discovers that a drayman is the culprit. Alan Howard announces that he is solvent again.

FEBRUARY

The twins are taken to Glasgow after Val's funeral. Ken stays at Weatherfield's Bay Tree Hotel, to get away for a while, where he is comforted by understanding receptionist Yvonne Chapel. The flats are demolished because of the structural fault which killed Val, and a new Community Centre and Warehouse are to be built on the site.

Billy Walker borrows Weatherfield's Mayoral Rolls to take Alan, Elsie and Irma for a joy-ride. On the return journey they hit a Mini outside a chip shop.

MARCH

Miss Nugent tries to organize a demonstration against building the Warehouse, but it fails through lack of support. She forms a human barricade and is covered in sand from a dumper.

Ken Barlow engages housekeeper Margaret Lacey to look after the twins. Lucille recognizes her as the nurse who ill-treated her at the orphanage, and she is forced to resign. Elsie accuses Alan of playing around, but the woman was simply a client buying a car.

APRIL

Annie Walker takes a cruise to Greece with local butcher Arthur Dewhurst, and returns alone saying she had a wonderful time. Arthur follows later, and to Billy Walker's outrage is accompanied by his attractive daughter-in-law.

Ray and Irma find Stan Ogden asleep in a van at his job as night watchman at Hulme's Bakery. They drive the van into town for a joke and park it. Stan is given his cards, but Ray offers him a job to make up for it.

MAY

Elsie is appointed supervisor at the Warehouse, despite Hilda telling the manager that she has been in court for theft. Hetty Thorpe, the new Community Centre caretaker, is frightened out of the job by Ena's tales of hooliganism. Ena promptly takes over. Ray Langton tries to sell portable saunas by getting Irma to pose as a French lady demonstrator.

JUNE

Stan, who feels he is being exploited at the yard, forms his own union, SODU – the Stanley Ogden District Union. When Len finds that Stan is being paid £1 more than the union rate, he cuts his wages. Emily feels that working with Ernest in the shop is endangering their relationship, and starts work at the Warehouse.

Billy Walker meets physiotherapist Lorna Shorecross when his mother invited her to lodge at the Rovers. He was about to propose when she left to marry her fiancé to whom she was secretly engaged.

JULY

Emily breaks off her friendship with Ernest because of a cartoon he has drawn of Annie for the local paper, but they make up and become engaged. Hilda's old flame, gardener George Greenwood, judges a flower show at the Community Centre and recognizes Stan's entry as an orchid stolen from the park. Minnie and Ena sample the home-made wine entries. Billy Walker moves to a self-service petrol station in Chiswick, leaving Alan Howard to manage the garage.

AUGUST

The Ogdens buy a colour TV, but two weeks later the HP company repossesses it. Ernest Bishop loses Emily's £100 engagement ring. Stan is suspected of stealing it, but it is found in his trouser turn-up. Former town hall clerk Janet Reid, now working at the Corner Shop, has a secret date with Alan Howard in Leeds. She tells everyone she is visiting her sister in Leicester, but Elsie finds out. Emily and Ernest hold an engagement party.

SEPTEMBER

Alan and Elsie are reconciled. Dave Smith takes Minnie for a day out to Blackpool to celebrate her birthday. Ernest Bishop leaves on a photographic assignment to Spain.

Hilda, in her quest for one-upmanship, orders Stan to build a serving hatch between the kitchen and living room. Stan gets the plans wrong and makes one big enough for a factory canteen. Hilda proudly throws a party to show it off to the neighbours, but only Ena turns up.

OCTOBER

Ken Barlow has an affair with hotel
receptionist Yvonne Chapel. He proposes, but
she turns him down, unable to cope with
looking after the twins. Jerry Booth returns to
the Street jobless and moves in with Len and
Ray. He knocks a customer unconscious in an
argument in the Rovers, and is given twelve
months conditional discharge. Ernest Bishop is
arrested photographing a sex orgy in Spain,
and charged with offending public morality.

NOVEMBER

Emily flies to Spain to plead for Ernest, while
Annie petitions the embassy officials. Behind
her back, Lucille becomes a go-go dancer at the
Aquarius Club. Irma Barlow begins dating
county footballer Eddie Duncan.

DECEMBER

Annie Walker goes to the Licensed Victuallers
Boxing Day Ball with Kitty Stonely, of the
Robin Hood, and Nellie Harvey. Annie is
offended by Bernard Manning's jokes, but
meets handsome widower Lt. Com. Gerald
Prince R.N.Ret., and a liaison starts.

Footballer Eddie transfers his attentions to
Bet Lynch. Hilda wins £500 on the Premium
Bonds and pays off the money borrowed from
Dave Smith to buy Irma's Corner Shop
partnership.

JANUARY

Ken Barlow is appointed Deputy Head at Bessie Street School, under Wilfred Perkins. Annie has a lunch date with Commander Prince, and invites him to the Rovers for an intimate dinner. There can be no romance between them, she tells him.

Football director Dave Smith sells Eddie Duncan to Torquay United. He leaves without Bet, but Irma follows him. Billy Walker sells his share in the garage to Alan for £2,500. A bearded Ernest Bishop returns from Spain.

FEBRUARY

Stan promises Hilda a trip to Paris for her birthday. They miss the plane and spend the day in the airport, but pretend they have been abroad. To Wilfred Perkins' disapproval, Ken Barlow strikes up an acquaintance with Rita Bates, whose son Terry is a pupil. Albert Tatlock is appointed assistant caretaker at the Community Centre, after a break-in in which a colour TV is stolen. Betty and Cyril Turpin offer to buy Irma's share in the Corner Shop from Maggie. She turns them down and borrows money from her son Gordon to buy it herself.

MARCH

Jerry Booth builds an 11 ft sailing dinghy, *Shangri-la*, in Len's yard. With Ray and Stan aboard, it capsizes on its maiden voyage. Elsie's eleven-year-old grandson, Paul Cheveski, stays with her for a short holiday. Emily, due to be married, refuses to move to Eccles.

APRIL

Ernest and Emily are married on Easter Monday at Mawdesley Street Congregational Church. Mavis Riley, Emily's workmate at the Mark Brittain Warehouse, is bridesmaid. After a reception at the Rovers the couple honeymoon in Edale. Mavis begins a friendship with Jerry Booth, and the Bishops return to set up home at No. 3. Ken moves out to live next door with Albert Tatlock.

MAY

Ken's headmaster learns that he is becoming more involved with Mrs Bates, and warns him to end the relationship. Len immediately starts an affair with her and discovers that she is not married to Harry Bates, and is not Terry's mother.

Stan, now a lorry driver, has had an accident delivering bananas to Newcastle. Hilda's brother Archie Crabtree moves in during Stan's absence and delights Hilda by building a porch over the front door. He is told to remove it because there was no planning permission. Stan returns from hospital and opens a window-cleaning round with a borrowed handcart.

JUNE

Elsie's £300 endowment policy – taken out when Dennis was a baby – matures, and she has a pink bathroom suite installed at No. 11. Stan draws up a territorial agreement with his tough window-cleaning rivals, the Henshaws, and ends up with a demolished street.

Maggie has a new assistant, Norma Ford, and is suspicious about the conflicting stories she tells. Maggie discovers that Norma's father is not in hospital, as she claims, but in prison. Len resumes his relationship with 'Mrs Bates', who is singing at the New Victoria Working Men's Club under her own name, Rita Littlewood.

JULY

Benny Lewis opens a new betting shop in Dave Smith's old premises. Emily and Ena ask him to restrict Minnie's betting because of her gambling problem. When Hilda takes a job at the betting shop cleaning, Annie sacks her from the Rovers.

Alan Howard's ex-wife Laura calls, offering to wipe off the debt of £2,000 he borrowed to buy the garage. Elsie insists that they will pay it in full.

AUGUST

Bookie Benny Lewis proposes to Rita Littlewood, and she accepts, but later jilts him for Len Fairclough. Lucille, Hilda, Emily and Elsie each become victims of a peeping-tom. A Street vigilante committee catches Stan in suspicious circumstances, but he is cleared when a man is charged.

Maggie Clegg meets draughtsman Ron Cooke through a lonely hearts ad which Norma placed without her knowledge. She stops seeing him when he confesses to being an ex-alcoholic.

SEPTEMBER

Ena is on the Street outing to Preston Guild when her grandson Colin Lomax and his wife Karen call from West Hartlepool. Their baby Jason is kidnapped from outside the Rovers, but found by Emily Bishop and Betty Turpin.

Alf Roberts' wife Phyllis dies in hospital. Lucille finds Annie depressed and suspects that she has taken an overdose. The hospital uses a stomach pump, but discovers that she has only had four tablets. Tommy Deakin and Dirty Dick dispute the ownership of Dolores the donkey.

OCTOBER

Weatherfield Pub Olympics: Stan Ogden wins a beer drinking contest against Piggy Owen of the Flying Horse. Concepta Hewitt arrives from Ireland to visit Lucille with her new fiancee Sean Regan.

Ray Langton lends Sharon Duffy, barmaid at the Vine, the keys to bookie Benny's flat to impress her. She arranges for her boyfriend to burgle the place, and £5,000 is missing.

NOVEMBER

Jacko Ford is arrested for the burglary and remanded to Risley after Hilda admits that she once showed him round Benny's penthouse flat. Concepta returns to Ireland with Sean, unaware that he made a pass at Bet Lynch.

Rita sings at the newly-open Capricorn Club, opened by Alan Howard, Jimmy Frazer and Benny Lewis. A tipsy woman calls her a 'brass-faced bitch' for dancing with her husband, and Rita hits her across the face.

DECEMBER

Hilda, reinstated at the Rovers, now has three cleaning jobs – the pub, the betting shop and the Capricorn. Stan contemplates retirement. Len and Alf Roberts are both in the running as next Mayor of Weatherfield. Everyone takes part in Ernest and Emily's '1940s Show' on Christmas Day. Annie, not unexpectedly, plays the part of Brittania.

Stan is accused of co-habiting with the lady from 19 Inkerman Street, and her social security benefit is stopped. Hilda clears his name and ends the affair for good.

149

JANUARY

Ken and Norma find evidence to corroborate Jacko's alibi, and he is freed from the burglary charge. Alf Roberts is made Mayor-elect and asks Maggie to become his Mayoress. She refuses, but Annie eagerly accepts. Alan Howard has a drink problem and comes to blows with Elsie. They make up and plan a new start. Lucille, fed up with Annie, moves in with them.

Minnie, deeply upset, finds a love letter from her late husband Armisted to Ena. Ena explains that she once had a tiff with Armisted and advised him to propose to Minnie. He did, and wrote to Ena to thank her.

FEBRUARY

Hilda celebrates her forty-ninth birthday with a Barbara Cartland-style party. Billy Walker is caught in Stan's bedroom with Edna Gee, and mistaken for Ernest Bishop. Ernest is too drunk and incapable to establish his innocence.

Alf Roberts gives Bet Lynch a late-night lift and knocks down an old lady, who is unhurt. Her crooked son tries to blackmail Alf for £200, but Bet gets the cheque back.

MARCH

Albert is taken to hospital because of a gas leak when Jerry Booth takes out his old cooker to install an electric model. The Street has to be evacuated to the Community Centre. The Capricorn Club is taken over by Duggie Bowker, who runs blue film shows. American Army Master Sergeant Mike Ritchie, a buddy of the late Steve Tanner, turns up to see his old flame Maggie Clegg.

150

APRIL

Mike goes home to a widow in Wichita, leaving Alf Roberts jealous of his attentions to Maggie, who is angry at his interference. Emily is jealous too, when Ernest asks Rita to tout for photographic orders on a commission basis. She outshines her by taking pictures of strippers at a local club.

Retiring Mayoress Ethel Bostock calls on Annie who mistakes her for the new charlady. Albert is challenged by an old school chum, retired teacher Herbert 'Jesse' James to walk the Pennine Way. Stan and Hilda have mice. On a tip-off from Elsie, the public health inspector fumigates the house. Hilda tries to uncover the informer.

MAY

Alf Roberts and Annie Walker are installed Mayor and Mayoress. Caterers refuse to supply the celebration party because Billy Walker's cheque has bounced. Annie, finding he has gambled with the Rovers accounts, puts Betty in charge.

Len buys Biddulph's shop in Rosamund Street, christens it the Kabin and installs Rita as manageress. Annie, Stan and Hilda join a Street outing to Woburn Abbey, where Minnie buys a tea towel from the Duke of Bedford.

JUNE

Mavis Riley is taken on as Rita's assistant at the Kabin. They discover that Biddulph was selling porn under the guise of the *Pig Producer's Weekly*. Hilda enrols for ballroom dancing classes at the Community Centre. The Street pools syndicate wins a first dividend. Stan has forgotten to pass Bet, Elsie and Alan Howard's stake money on to Ray who refuses to share the winnings.

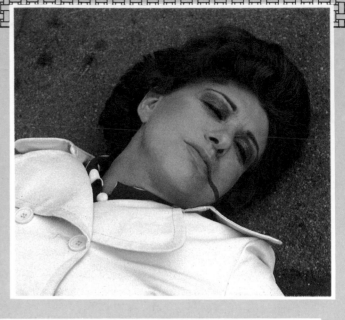

JULY

The pools win turns out to be £300. Ray decides to pay Bet, Alan and Elsie £75 each – and the Ogdens nothing. Bet is mugged on the way home from the Rovers, and taken to hospital. Stan is suspected, but has an alibi – he was at 19 Inkerman Street.

Elsie tells Alan she is going to see Sheila Birtles in Sheffield, but catches a train to London. She is visiting Dennis, who is in Pentonville prison for hustling double glazing to pensioners. Elsie is knocked down by a taxi in Oxford Street, and lies in hospital unidentified, suffering from concussion.

AUGUST

Elsie is traced to Guy's Hospital by the police, and Alan travels to visit her. She recovers enough to return home for the bank holiday, while the Street awaits the truth about her trip.

The men challenge the women to a bank holiday bowls match, and win. As a forfeit the girls stage a drag show in the Select.

SEPTEMBER

Annie Walker finds out about Dennis from Billy, but respects Elsie's wish for secrecy. Deirdre Hunt is taken on by Ray to work in the office at the Yard, and Jerry's initial disapproval melts. Alan Howard has a brawl with Stan after Hilda calls Elsie a slag. Ken Barlow starts an affair with Janet Reid.

OCTOBER

Ken brings the twins from Glasgow to meet Janet. Later they travel to meet Val's mother, who does not approve of Janet. Ena returns from holiday in Llandudno and finds she is threatened with dismissal at the Community Centre. She has a heart attack in the Snug.

A Street non-smoking syndicate, launched to buy a villa in Majorca, collapses. Ken and Janet arrive home from Glasgow and announce they have married at her parents' in Keswick.

NOVEMBER

Ken and Janet throw a wedding party at the Rovers, but the marriage gets off to a rocky start. Janet finds a house for £11,500, which Ken refuses to consider. They are late at the estate agent's to buy a house in Cheadle, and miss it. Ken slaps Janet's face in a furious row.

Annie, as Mayoress, invites volunteers to accommodate visitors from Weatherfield's twin town Charleville. Bet looks after Marcel Lebeque, anticipating romance. Stan and Hilda opt for a girl, Renee Dubois. 'She' turns out to be a huge juggernaut driver who becomes firm friends with Stan.

DECEMBER

Albert proposes to Minnie for financial reasons, but she tells him to ask Ena's permission first. Ena thinks Albert is proposing to her, and accepts. Ena is sacked by the Community Centre Committee for inefficiency. Minnie publicly accuses Committee members Ernest and Emily of evicting her, and the Street ostracizes them. On New Year's Eve, Ena moves to St Annes.

Rita announces that she intends to marry Len. Stan and Hilda visit their son Trevor and his wife Pauline in Chesterfield, and find that they have had a baby. Trevor has told his wife that his parents are dead, because he wants to go up in the world (wouldn't you?).

1974

FEBRUARY

Len refuses to attend a protest meeting against the redevelopment, and is sent to Coventry by everyone – except the Ogdens, who are property owners. Someone throws a brick through his window, unaware that he has voted against it. Emily sheepishly owns up.

Ken has his first big row with Janet because she wants to send the twins to boarding school. Albert breaks off his engagement, and Minnie is relieved because her pension would have been reduced. Cyril Turpin dies, leaving Betty mentally confused with grief.

JANUARY

Len reveals that the London Development Company intend to demolish the Street and redevelop it. Rita leaks the news to an aghast Rovers. Arthur Harvey, an old friend of Annie, stays at the Rovers and tells her that she has always been his secret love. His wife Nellie calls to find him in his pyjamas, and threatens to sue an outraged Annie for enticement.

Billy Walker returns and buys the garage from Alan Howard. Ken manages to arrange places for the twins at Bessie Street School. He meets Janet's ambitious friends, Jill and Phillip Barrett, and finds them 'inverted snobs'.

MARCH

Cyril leaves only £859, and Betty moves in with Maggie, hoping to sell the house. Hilda is shortlisted as caretaker for the Community Centre. The Committee are impressed with a gushing reference from Annie, but the job goes to Mrs Gertie Robson.

Ken and Janet decide to let the twins remain in Glasgow. Lucille reveals that she is living with mechanic Danny Burrows, a married man. Annie thinks she is staying with Lorraine Binks. Emily decides upon the dramatic society's next production: *The Importance of Being Ernest*.

APRIL

Annie Walker hands in her Mayoress's chain. Lucille leaves Danny after Annie invites him to tea and gives him the third degree. Mavis Riley takes a job as a vet's receptionist. Betty, unable to sell her house, returns to the Rovers.

Curtain up on *The Importance of Being Ernest*, with Annie as Lady Bracknell. Gary Turner, Mrs Robson's nephew, moves in with her at the Centre. Stan gets Hilda an application form for a job aboard a luxury cruise liner.

MAY

With the help of Annie's well-worn reference, Hilda passes the interview and joins the Seamen's union. She sails on the *MV Monte Umbe*, leaving Mrs Robson to monitor Stan's movements in the vicinity of 19 Inkerman Street.

Warehouse chief Sir Julius Berlin, impressed at Ken's handling of the redevelopment protest, offers him a job. When Ken refuses, Janet walks out on him, but he reconsiders and takes the offer. Alf Roberts helps Maggie out in the Corner Shop.

JUNE

Stan has taken in lodgers Tommy Deakin and his nephew Michael Ryan, and is breathalysed driving a Rolls they borrowed. The lodgers quit, leaving Stan with a donkey, the mainstay of their garden manure business.

Hilda returns, but when Stan confesses his impending £200 fine, refuses to help. Maggie's old flame Ron Cooke, the reformed alcoholic, proposes. She turns down a counter-offer from Alf Roberts and accepts.

JULY

A young soldier, Martin Downes, calls at the Rovers trying to trace his long lost mother, called Elizabeth. He discovers that it is Bet Lynch but, appalled by her vulgarity, leaves without telling her.

Stan's £50 fine and £143 solicitor's bill leave Hilda with £7 from her cruise wages – and there is more bad luck to come. She asks Annie for a rise and gets the sack. Maggie Clegg marries Ron Cooke. Battleaxe Granny Hopkins and son Idris, the new Corner Shop owners, refuse Hilda credit. Ken Barlow leaves Bessie Street, with a presentation tankard and briefcase, for his new job. Gail Potter first appears in the Street, as a clerk at the Warehouse. Vera Hopkins, Idris's wife, leaves after a row with Granny.

AUGUST

Stan and Hilda are offered the caretakership of the Centre, and put their house up for sale. The Council withdraw the offer in view of the Ogden's record with the Health Department. Annie takes Hilda back with a small wage increase.

Ken faces his first test when unions at the Warehouse demand recognition. Billy Walker and Deirdre Hunt fall in love, then he meets her corset-fitter mum Blanche Hunt, who takes a fancy to him.

SEPTEMBER

Ray Langton goads Billy Walker about Deirdre, and the difference in their ages, and gets a black eye. Albert Tatlock is roughed-up by soccer hooligans at the Centre. Landlord Wormold's assistant Jimmy Graham falls for Rita and offers to leave his wife for her.

Stan and Hilda tell everyone they are going on a tandem holiday, but secretly leave the bike at the station and take the train to Morecambe. The porter sends it back while they are away, and they return embarrassed in their cycling togs on foot.

1974

156

OCTOBER

Deirdre and Billy agree to marry. The girls win a package holiday to Majorca on 'Place the Ball'. Mavis Riley is flustered by a Spaniard called Pedro, and Rita falls for a bronzed beach boy. Bet lingers with a property con-man and misses the plane. Annie returns to find that Billy is serving after-hours drinks in the Rovers.

At the garage, Billy services a van crammed with stolen suede jackets from the Warehouse. Billy is arrested and spends a night in the cells. Ken secures his release by obtaining a confession from the father of one of the young thieves.

NOVEMBER

Marital problems lead to separate beds for Emily and Ernest. They decide to become foster parents and temporarily take in two black children whose father is in hospital. Ken, still sorting out shop-floor problems at the Warehouse, falls for union organizer Peggy Barton. Billy Walker reveals that he lent Bet the £70 air fare to get home from Majorca – the money he had saved to buy a ring for Deirdre.

DECEMBER

For a joke, Bet persuades her Spanish neighbour Carlos to call Mavis and impersonate Pedro, her holiday lover. He asks for a date, but confesses the hoax; they spend Christmas together. Eddie Yeats, Jed Stone's Walton cell-mate, arrives to spend the holiday with Minnie, and cashes in on a power cut by selling cut-price candles at the Rovers.

Granny Hopkins finds a birth certificate in the back of a Corner Shop drawer which shows that Gordon Clegg's mother is Betty Turpin, not Maggie. As the sale of the shop is still going through, she tries to use it to lever a lower price.

JANUARY

Eddie Yeats returns to Walton in a prison van for overstaying his Christmas parole. Carlos proposes to Mavis, who sends him packing when she finds he is really looking for a residency permit.

Battered wife Lynn Johnson calls on Councillor Fairclough for advice, and is found dead in his living room. Len is held by murder squad detectives, but released when the husband confesses.

FEBRUARY

Granny Hopkins sends Gordon Clegg a nasty letter revealing his real parentage, but Maggie has already told him. He tears up the Corner Shop sale contract, and the Hopkins leave under cover of darkness in Cox's Removals van.

Alf Roberts asks Rita to partner him to entertain a visiting alderman and his wife. He is embarrassed when Rita wears a plunging dress, but Alderman Digby's wife Dawn wears one equally revealing. Ray Langton sends Stan a Valentine from the lady at 19 Inkerman Street. Hilda storms round to confront her, and makes a fool of herself.

MARCH

Len has an on-off relationship with Bet Lynch. Stan Ogden has been in hospital with middle-ear trouble. He returns to find his social security benefit cut, and Hilda takes over the window-cleaning round. Eddie Yeats helps Hilda, and together they make £4 more than Stan's normal wage.

Betty Turpin wins Newton and Ridley's 'Personality of the Pub' competition. Billy shows Deirdre his £526 savings, and they name the day – a June wedding with top-hat, tails and all the trimmings.

APRIL

Bad news for Bet: she ends the affair with Len when he refuses to live with her, and learns that her illegitimate son Martin has been killed in a Belfast road accident. Eddie Yeats encourages her to turn up for work at the Rovers and washes her tights at the laundrette because she has nothing to wear. Bet is touched by his kindness.

Annie Walker and Blanche Hunt discover they have bought identical daffodil wedding outfits. Stan Ogden and Eddie Yeats buy a dishevelled dog called Fury and branch into the guard dog business. Albert agrees to keep it in his back yard.

MAY

Gail Potter applies for an air hostess's job, making Deirdre unsettled at the prospect of being tied by marriage. The engagement ends. Fury guards Len's yard, but a thief breaks in and steals £200 worth of copper piping – and the dog.

Rita sings at the Gatsby Club while, in the audience, Ray Langton brawls with a drunken oil rigger. Billy Walker leaves to manage the Hotel Carlotta in Jersey. Ernest Bishop and Alf Roberts are at loggerheads over the rates, prompting Ernest to form WARP – Weatherfield Association of Ratepayers.

JUNE

A fight breaks out when Ernest tries to record Len's views on the rates on a tape recorder. Ernest wrongly accuses a councillor of corruption and has to apologize on Radio Weatherfield. Ken Barlow is now a taxi-driver, and Annie objects to him using the Rovers telephone to take bookings.

Mavis buys two gross of misshapen tights from a con-man – each pair has one leg shorter than the other. Deirdre resigns from the Yard office after a blazing row with Langton, but the hate turns to love . . . and thoughts of marriage.

JULY

After a joint stag and hen party at the Rovers, Deirdre and Ray marry at Weatherfield Register Office. Len throws a surprise champagne reception. They miss their train and have to spend their wedding night at Blanche Hunt's. Albert Tatlock goes to hospital to have a 'floating' piece of shrapnel removed from his bottom. He proudly shows the memento round the Rovers.

Brassy Post Office canteen girl Donna Parker calls on Alf Roberts late at night, saying she has been thrown out of her flat. He takes her in and lends her £500 to start a hairdressing business. The lady vanishes.

AUGUST

The Street holds a party for Albert's eightieth birthday, and the Lancashire Fusiliers send a bugler. Ken Barlow enrols at a computer dating agency and is paired with a shocked Mavis, who joined under an assumed name.

Is the ghost of Martha Longhurst haunting the Rovers? The regulars call her on a Ouija board to no avail. After the great rates uproar, Stan and Hilda discover that they are the only house to withhold their payments. The rating officer investigates.

SEPTEMBER

A fare Ken picks up in his taxi turns out to be his estranged wife Janet and Vince Denton, the man she is living with. Ken invites them home and they get on well together. Newly-wed Deirdre has a party, but throws everyone out when someone burns her new coffee table with a cigarette.

Eddie Yeats is arrested for handling stolen property. Three young hooligans wreck the Centre. Ken calls at their home to remonstrate, but refuses to call the police. Society is to blame, he says. Albert reports them and the boys break Ken's windows, thinking he has shopped them.

OCTOBER

The three delinquents break into the Warehouse and leave a cigarette smouldering in an armchair. There is a huge blaze and the Street has to be evacuated as the flames approach liquid gas tanks. Rovers regulars take refuge in the New Old Inn.

Next day, when the all-clear is sounded, Annie returns to find her nest-egg of thirty-five gold sovereigns missing. Billy had moved them for safety, leaving Annie ashamed that she had suspected her customers. A drunken Gordon Clegg lets slip the secret that Betty is his mother to a barmaid. Soon the news is all round the Street.

NOVEMBER

Betty finds it hard to face the Rovers. Ken Barlow is appointed Community Development Officer. His first project, a Bonfire Night reading of the history of the Gunpowder Plot, without fireworks, is a flop.

A distressed Len receives news of the death of Jerry Booth. Concepta's Irish husband Sean visits the Rovers and tries to kiss Bet. She allows him – then smacks him across the face and threatens to tell Concepta what a rat she married. Annie Walker is taken to hospital after being terrorized by two youths after closing time. Len and Ray intervene and beat them up.

DECEMBER

Deirdre blacks Tricia Hopkins' eye for spreading a rumour that Ray is having an affair with a blonde housewife, Pauline Jarvis. The Rovers Amateur Dramatic Society perform *Cinderella*. Len is Buttons, Bet as Prince Charming mimes *When I Fall In Love*, with Rita singing in the wings. Tricia plays the title role with a black eye.

Hilda's son Trevor arrives to take her to Chesterfield, where Polly is expecting a new baby. Hilda refuses to leave until the panto is over.

JANUARY

Blanche Hunt leaves with Dave Smith to manage his new country club, and hands the Corner Shop keys to Betty. Hilda returns to tell Stan about his new granddaughter Jayne, and notices that he is looking well-fed. She suspects the reason lies at 19 Inkerman Street, but Minnie Caldwell has been cooking for him.

Tricia Hopkins starts a rumour that Mission Fund treasurer Ernest Bishop has embezzled £5. Ernest, who has merely mislaid a postal order, rebukes everyone for their lack of charity. The fire-raising hooligans get three months detention.

FEBRUARY

A month of misunderstanding. An anonymous letter to the Town Hall alleges that Alf Robert's expensive new watch is a planning bribe from Dave Smith. Len and Rita trick Donna Parker into parting with £500 by pretending to sell the Kabin as a hairdressing salon, to repay the money she conned from Alf. An angry Alf reveals that Donna not only repaid the cash, but gave him the watch.

Annie is caught by the TV detector van. Hilda panics and buys a licence, unknown to Stan who tries to hide the set and drops it. Believing that the rental company replace sets damaged by fire, he sets it alight. The firm sends them a £75 bill for damages. Albert sits as a model at the Centre's new art classes.

MARCH

Stan and Hilda win a chance to fill a supermarket trolley with as much as they can in one minute. Stan's back gives way, and Deirdre has to deputize. Ken becomes attracted to married graduate Wendy Nightingale, who conducts a survey on reading habits at the Centre. They spend the night together when her husband is away.

Mavis returns from a weekend in Kendal with Derek Wilton. She refuses to elaborate, but a mood-stone ring he has given her turns green, signifying contentment. Stan is missing: Hilda draws a blank at 19 Inkerman Street, and finds he has been accidentally locked in the Rovers cellar with Albert Tatlock. Annie, whose stocks are depleted after the incident, takes on a resident bar-cellarman, Fred Gee.

APRIL

Wendy's suspicious husband bursts into No. 11 and assaults Ken. The brewery runs a Super-Brain Contest, and Stan wins the heat to represent the Rovers. Confidence is low, so he is plied with beer and sent to the wrong venue. Bet, as substitute, goes through to the finals.

Elsie returns to the Street and becomes manageress at Sylvia's Separates. Ernest Bishop lets his standards slip and goes on a strippers-and-booze night out with Alf and Ray, forgetting it is his wedding anniversary. The club is raided, and the story splashed across the *Weatherfield Gazette*. Emily locks Ernest out. Ken organizes a Spring Bank Holiday party with roundabouts, Punch and Judy and refreshments. Stan does an escapology act, but is too fat to free himself.

MAY

Bet loses the Super-Brain final, but goes out with the question master. Wendy Nightingale moves in briefly with Ken, but decides to go back to her husband when the Committee threatens his livelihood. Fred Gee falls for Rita, and gives her a single red rose. Renee Bradshaw makes Gordon an offer for the Corner Shop, and takes over for three weeks trial.

JUNE

Ken moves in with Albert, and Elsie goes back to her old house No. 11. Gail Potter, sacked from the shop by Renee Bradshaw, joins her. Eddie Yeats returns, looking for digs, and joker Ray directs him to No. 11. Elsie finds Eddie and his pal, Monkey Gibbon, sleeping in her bed, and attacks Ray with her handbag in the Rovers.

Renee is reported for Sunday trading. She accuses Emily, but discovers it was Tricia Hopkins. Ray plans a wedding anniversary party at the Rovers and gives Annie £25 deposit. Deirdre, who wants to buy a house, insists that he cancels it.

JULY

The Ogdens invite Eddie to lodge with them. He offers to decorate, but runs out of paper. To fill in the gaps he buys a scenic vista of the Alps, delighting Hilda who wants to out-do Annie Walker with her 'muriel'. Ray announces that Deirdre is pregnant. Ernest is broke and Emily sells her engagement ring to pay the bills.

Albert wins £100 at bingo. Fred Gee obtains Annie's permission to entertain a lady friend at the Rovers. She is horrified when he arrives with Vera Duckworth.

AUGUST

Ernest has to turn down a hospital porter's job – the sight of blood makes him squeamish. Annie decides to learn to drive when she hears that Nellie Harvey has passed her test after eighty-six lessons. Ernest gets a pianist's job on stag nights at the Gatsby. Emily is upset when a stripper calls round to practise.

Len's tools are stolen from a building site by rough labourer Jack Barker. He doctors some scaffolding so that Len will fall. It collapses under Ray and Len brawls with Barker. Mavis Riley has tea with Derek's disapproving mum, who says they must stop seeing each other.

SEPTEMBER

Gail Potter, cited in a divorce, is sacked from Sylvia's Separates. Elsie wins back her job for her. Fred Gee buys a greyhound and keeps it secretly in Annie's cellar. There are accusations all round when Annie, out for a driving lesson, swerves to avoid the dog and crashes into Stan Ogden's handcart.

Ken discovers that Eddie Yeats has a natural ability with children, and offers him a job as playleader. He is forced to quit when parents do not take kindly to an ex-jailbird supervising their offspring.

OCTOBER

Annie loses a court battle against Renee Bradshaw's application for an off-licence. Minnie's house, No. 5, goes up for sale. Mike Baldwin opens a new warehouse and goes into the shirt and jeans business, taking Ernest Bishop on as pay clerk.

Hilda, already furious that the old mac she left in the Rovers has been used on a guy, discovers that Stan has taken £6 from her Christmas savings. She throws him out. Rita knocks Len from a barstool in the Gatsby in a row over a singing engagement, and he cracks his head. The doctor says he is fine, but he feigns illness, forcing Rita and Elsie to dance attendance. Rita finds out the truth and pours a pint of beer over him.

NOVEMBER

Stan, reported missing by a worried Hilda, turns up at his brother-in-law Norman's chip shop, where Norman's 'fancy woman' takes a liking to him. A livid Hilda drags him home.

Mike Baldwin buys No. 5, and Bet Lynch moves in as his 'housekeeper'. Mavis has literary leanings and writes a novel based on the Street. *Song of a Scarlet Summer* – a semi bodice-ripper – uses characters with the same initials as locals: Stan Ogden, for instance, becomes Santos Olivia.

DECEMBER

Sylvia's Separates goes up for sale. Mike Baldwin buys it as a retail outlet, but tells Elsie she is too old to sell trendy clothes. She moves to the factory as supervisor. Wage clerk Ernest Bishop refuses to change pay day to Thursdays. The girls de-bag him at the Christmas party, and hand his trousers to a frosty Emily.

Annie passes her driving test, and buys a second hand Rover 2000 from Eddie Yeats' crooked pal Lanky Potts. Annie is breathalysed after a Licensed Victuallers' luncheon. The reading is positive, but a blood sample clears her. Mike Baldwin, suffused with Christmas spirit, gives Bet the keys to No. 5. Hilda gets a new mac from Stan.

1977

JANUARY

After a false alarm, Deirdre's baby arrives. Suzie Birchall is taken on to help Gail Potter at Mike Baldwin's shop. Ernest rows with Emily and goes to a dance at the Centre alone. He meets enthusiastic spinster Thelma James, and takes her home. Bet gives a girl who is chasing Mike Baldwin a black eye on the dance floor.

Eddie Yeats and Monkey Gibbon are hoaxed by Bet about cheap watches they are hawking. She tells them the police are making enquiries, and they hastily stuff them down a grid before she can stop them. They race back to find council workmen emptying the drain into a tanker.

FEBRUARY

Hilda wisely insists that Stan changes their house number from unlucky 13 to 12A. The Council makes him change it back under an Act of 1847. Mike Baldwin clinches a rag trade deal by persuading Bet and a reluctant Betty Turpin to entertain a business contact.

Emily confronts Ernest with a Valentine he receives from spinster Thelma James. Janet Barlow pleads with Ken to take her back. He refuses, but allows her to stay the night. Next day he finds her dead from an overdose.

MARCH

Mike Baldwin orders Bet out of No. 5 – his wife is arriving unexpectedly. Bet finds that they are not married, and refuses to move. Mike sells the house to the Langtons, and Bet moves to the Corner Shop flat. She ruins Renee's stock by accidentally turning off the freezer, and works behind the counter to pay off the loss.

Suzie Birchall and Gail Potter try to sweep Elsie's chimney with a brick on a rope, and fill the Ogden's with soot. Rita is leaving for a singing engagement in Teneriffe, when Len proposes. She turns him down, but changes her mind at the airport, and the plane leaves without her.

APRIL

Len and Rita are married at St Margaret's, Weatherfield, to a background of Elgar and Wagner. For the reception at the Greenvale Hotel, the mood music changes to Victor Sylvester. Deirdre wants a christening for Tracey, but the vicar refuses because they are not church-goers.

Fred Gee and Alf Roberts take Mavis and Renee out fishing. Renee loses her footing and falls in the river, and Fred tumbles after her, trying to retrieve his rod. Alf and Mavis attempt a rescue, but are pulled in after them.

MAY

Mike Baldwin offers a trendy denim suit for a new name for Sylvia's Separates. Albert Tatlock suggests 'the Western Front', and wins. The vicar relents and Tracey is christened at St Margaret's. Mavis moves into the Kabin flat, and Len and Rita have their first big row – he had planned to let it for a high rental.

Ken Barlow has difficulty organizing a float for the Jubilee celebrations. Annie offers to borrow one from the brewery – on condition that she plays Elizabeth I. Elsie has a visitor: Elaine Dennett calls from Newcastle to say she is in love with Alan, who wants a divorce.

JUNE

Jubilee Day: HGV driver Stan Ogden leaves the float lights on all night and drains the battery, leaving the cast of *Britain Through the Ages* stranded. It includes Annie as Elizabeth I, Ena as Victoria, Eddie as a cave man, Ken as Sir Edmund Hilary and Albert as Sherpa Tensing.

Ena, baby-sitting Tracey while Ray and Deirdre spend a weekend in London, falls and hits her head. The distraught Langtons return to find her in hospital, and Tracey with the Bishops at No. 3. Shop steward Ivy Tilsley threatens a strike when Mike Baldwin introduces a three-day week.

JULY

Ena's caring neighbours organize an hourly rota to look after her, but she stubbornly throws them all out. Bet and Renee are chatted up by two crooks who arrange to meet them at a non-existent house in Ashton. In their absence the pair steal £400 worth of stock from the Corner Shop.

Trouble at the Rovers: Brewery painters, sent to give the pub a face-lift, are sacked for doing a 'foreigner' at the Bishops. Draymen walk out in protest, and there is no beer. Stan and Eddie brew their own in the bath, and a worried Hilda pulls the plug out – before discovering that it is not illegal.

AUGUST

Betty Turpin storms out of the Rovers after being wrongly suspected of stealing £45. Mavis, nursing her Aunty Edie who is recovering from a heart attack, reluctantly agrees to a night out with boyfriend Derek Wilton, and returns to find Edie dead.

Ken is winched by helicopter from a gulley while hiking on Kinder Scout. Annie agrees to buy a carpet, monogrammed AW, from Eddie Yeats at £5 a yard. Stan sells the Ogden's tandem for £7, then discovers it is worth £100 as an antique. Eddie buys it back but leaves it in a derelict house which is demolished, burying it completely.

SEPTEMBER

Ken limps home with torn ligaments. Annie invites her Lady Licensed Victuallers friends to a sherry party to show off her new carpet. To her mortification it has come from the local bingo hall. AW stands for Alhambra, Weatherfield.

Warehouse van driver Steve Fisher takes Gail and Suzie on a delivery to Southport. The van sinks on the sands and Mike Baldwin threatens him with the sack. Len and Rita row over her singing career. She agrees to one more date at the Gatsby.

OCTOBER

Hilda wins a 'Second Honeymoon Competition' run by Loving Cup Shandies. Her slogan: 'Be a mistress as well as a wife, and your husband will be a boyfriend.' Deirdre is molested under the Viaduct, but refuses to report the attack to the police.

The factory girls, under Ivy Tilsley, threaten to strike when Mike Baldwin promotes his new girlfriend. A drunken Alf Roberts proposes to Renee Bradshaw in the Gatsby, and she accepts. Alf, sobering rapidly, talks his way out of it.

NOVEMBER

Annie, celebrating forty years at the Rovers, meets a con-man who purports to be one of the Beaumonts of Clitheroe, and sends him packing. Stan and Hilda enjoy their 'Second Honeymoon' prize – a night in a four-star hotel with £25 to spend.

A stressful Deirdre walks out on Ray and the baby, and contemplates suicide on a motorway parapet. A lorry driver stops to ask directions, and brings her back to reality. She returns wearily home. Derek Wilton offers to take out a joint mortgage with Mavis.

DECEMBER

Christmas: Mike Baldwin throws a party at the factory and Hilda, thinking it is fancy dress, goes as Charlie Chaplin. Alf and Albert are invited to Annie Walker's for Boxing Day lunch, where they dine cautiously on Old English Jellied Rabbit. Rita invites Elsie for a 'slimming meal', while Eddie Yeats tries to sell a dubious consignment of late turkeys.

Fred Gee, thinking Len is two-timing Rita, knocks him out at Deirdre's New Year party, breaking her prized coffee table. Derek Wilton pulls out of the joint mortgage and says he is being transferred to Birkenhead. Mavis suspects his mother is behind it.

JANUARY

Hilda camps out all night for a £5 colour TV in Perkins' January sales. She is so keen to be interviewed on local radio that she loses her place in the queue, and the bargain. Annie commands Fred to get the Rover a quick MOT and chauffeur her and a party of Lady Licensed Victuallers to Southport. Bet borrows Ken's taxi-driver's peaked cap for him.

Ernest Bishop is murdered by shotgun raiders during a wage snatch at the Warehouse. He dies on the operating table. After the funeral Emily goes away to be alone with her grief.

FEBRUARY

Ken Barlow dates Albert's chiropodist, divorcee Sally Robson. Gail, Suzie and Elsie suspect they have rats in the rafters. They turn out to be pigeons, which have gained entry through a missing slate in the Ogden's roof. Suzie's foot slips through the Odgen's ceiling and Hilda retaliates by pushing a broom through Elsie's. The Small Claims Court rules that they each pay for their own repairs.

Alf proposes again to Renee, but she confides in Rita that she wants to be loved for herself, not the shop. When Alf hears this from Len he tells her he loves her, and she accepts.

MARCH

Suzie Birchall runs into trouble for using Mike Baldwin's phone to ring a boyfriend in France. Alf and Renee are married and spend their honeymoon in Capri. Len spends the night in jail for being drunk and disorderly at Alf's stag party. Ernest's killers get life imprisonment.

Elsie receives her decree nisi from Alan and goes out on the town. After being picked up by a commercial traveller who mistakes her for a tart, she goes away to think things over. Ena returns to find the Snug taken over by Albert's British Legion chums, but quickly reasserts herself. Ken Barlow annoys Gail and Suzie by picking an Easter Bonnet Competition winner from another street to prove he is not biased.

APRIL

Len is dropped as Ratepayers candidate after his night in the cells. Rita, angry at his suggestive remarks to the WPC who arrested him, locks him out of the bedroom. Stan is jokingly squirted with perfume by Bet, and Hilda suspects him of infidelity.

Mavis tells Derek a few home truths when he breaks the news that his mother has selected a wife for him. Alf and Renee, back from honeymoon, have difficulty removing Bet from the Corner Shop flat.

MAY

Ken organizes a bank holiday Lancashire Night at the Rovers, while Annie is in Jersey. Police, investigating the theft of her Rover, book everyone for drinking after hours. Annie returns deeply shocked, but her Rover is recovered with a note on the windscreen: 'Your tappets need adjusting.'

The Flying Horse challenges the Rovers to a sponsored pram race. Eddie, pushed by Mavis, gives up and is blackballed from the Rovers. He goes to the Flying Horse to share their winning barrel of beer, but is banned from there too.

JUNE

Fred Gee is told by brewery chief Richard Cresswell that he can take over the Mechanics Arms – providing he has a wife. He is turned down by Bet, Betty, and Alma Walsh, the barmaid at the Flying Horse.

Hilda asks Mike Baldwin for a new brush, and is promptly sacked for damaging her existing broom. The factory is ringed by pickets and Mike tries to bring in non-union labour. Elsie returns and passes the word around that she wishes to be known as Elsie Tanner again.

JULY

Mike Baldwin climbs down and offers Hilda her job back. Alf Roberts, upset at the prospect of his mother-in-law moving in, asks Bet to stay. Len is in debt when a contractor goes broke. He launches an emergency plumbing service, and Rita goes back to singing.

Ena cannot afford to replace her forty-year-old bed, but refuses to accept charity. Eddie, Len, Ray and Emily break in and install a new one. Ena, miffed but grateful, tells them, tongue-in-cheek, that her life savings were in the mattress. Well-meaning Emily takes in a battered wife, who eventually rejoins her husband and turns on Emily.

AUGUST

Stan and Eddie hope for big money cleaning stained glass windows. They clean St Margaret's, where the vicar thanks them for their charity and arranges for them to clean St Chad's as well. Baker Joe Dawson opens a cafe next door to the Kabin, employing Emily as manageress.

Annie Walker vies with Bet to be photographed for the cover of the new brewery magazine. The editor, to Annie's horror, opts for a picture of Eddie and Betty Turpin at the bar. Hilda, disgusted at her high water rates, insists that Stan takes a bath each day to get their money's-worth. The bath overflows, ruining her Alpine 'muriel'. She replaces it with a seascape to complement the plaster ducks.

SEPTEMBER

Ken's son Peter arrives to continue his education in Weatherfield. Albert blames an outbreak of food poisoning on Annie's pies. The problem is traced to vegetables from Albert's allotment which had been sprayed with insecticide.

Ray Langton dates Janice Stubbs, a black waitress from Dawson's Cafe. They decide to cool things in case Deirdre finds out. Elsie, who has a liaison with taxi-driver Ron Mather, hears that he has another woman, but she turns out to be a ballroom-dancing partner.

OCTOBER

Annie Walker, suffering with back trouble, is examined by a bogus doctor who is really no more than a hospital porter. 'He handled me!" she moans. Deirdre confronts Ray about his affair, and ponders her future. Ken Barlow reluctantly allows Peter to join the Navy.

Unknown to Hilda, Stan and Eddie rent out their handcart and go to the races with the proceeds. Hilda finds it parked and wheels it home, only to be stopped by a policeman who discovers that it is loaded with stolen lead.

NOVEMBER

Elsie goes to Majorca with taxi-man Ron, and is wooed with champagne by wealthy Oldham exile Harry Payne. Elsie warns a jealous Ron: if he tries to rule her life, there will be trouble. Deirdre's marriage is on the rocks – Ray takes a building job in Holland, leaving her alone with Tracey at No. 5.

Mike Baldwin decides it is too quiet on the Western Front, and closes the shop down. Eddie offers to help cook an Old Folk's Supper at the Centre, but burns the food. The chip shop is closed, so he collects tins from door to door and warms up a spaghetti supper.

DECEMBER

Suzie Birchall seeks her fortune in London. Illiterate Karen Barnes seeks reading lessons from Ken Barlow, who ignores advice that her jailbird husband is extremely jealous. Deirdre receives an ultimatum from Ray – join him, or sell the house. Brian Tilsley gatecrashes a party at Elsie's and makes a date with Gail.

JANUARY

Hilda, inspired by Christmas cards, takes up painting. Eddie cons Annie Walker into buying one of her pictures – by 'an unknown primitive artist' – for twenty guineas. On the back Annie stonily reads the message: 'Stan – am at bingo. Your dinner's in the oven.' Dave Barnes bursts into his wife's literacy lessons, threatening Ken and terrorizing Albert. Ken knocks him cold.

Ivy and Bert Tilsley buy No. 5 for £7,000. Suzie Birchall hitch-hikes home from London, broke, and signs up with a model agency. Annie walks into the Rovers, and is appalled to find Fred Gee taking bets. Len is found collapsed through overwork.

FEBRUARY

Len, recuperating, watches Rita sing *Birth of the Blues* at the Gatsby. Deirdre moves in with Emily, while Ivy and Bert – a Mantovani fan with interests in astronomy – take over No. 5. Stan cleans their windows by mistake, and Ivy refuses to pay. Hilda solves the impasse by throwing dirty water over them.

Brian Tilsley has an on-off affair with Gail. Elsie's Ron Mather leaves to take a chauffeur's job in Torquay. Bet Lynch, kidnapped in a rag stunt and held to £20 ransom, is slightly dismayed when the Rovers regulars raise only £4.56p to free her.

MARCH

Sally Norton, who was in maternity hospital with Deirdre, offers to take Tracey out in her pram. It is last seen outside the Rovers, before a lorry driver has a heart attack at the wheel and ploughs into the pub. Police and firemen tear at the rubble and find Tracey's doll. Deirdre runs hysterically from the Street, but the baby is found safe with Sally.

Mike Baldwin and Len are injured in the accident, and Alf Roberts lies unconscious in hospital for three weeks. Renee waits at his bedside throughout their wedding anniversary. Mike puts officious young Steve Fisher in sole command of the factory, and the girls threaten to walk-out. Mike discharges himself to sort out the trouble.

1979

APRIL

Brian Tilsley and Gail Potter throw an engagement party. To Gail's disappointment her vivacious, man-chasing mum is invited. Fred Gee, spurned by Mrs Potter, rethinks his image, and buys a wig. Alf, out of hospital, is displaying disturbing outbursts of temper with customers in the shop.

Eddie and Stan keep three hens in Hilda's back yard. Eddie christens them Hilda, Mrs Walker and Ena. Ken Barlow starts a jogging club and waits for recruits.

MAY

Suzie Birchall puts hard-boiled eggs in the Ogden's coop. Hilda proudly gives two eggs to Ena, who cuts one open in the Rovers, to Hilda's embarrassment. Only Mavis turns up for jogging, and Ken finds he is too out of condition to run. Alf insults more customers, and is sent for psychiatric treatment.

Ken abandons jogging for the dance floor, and invites Deirdre on a disco date. Billy Walker arrives home, and wastes no time in asking her out. Annie's Rover is towed to the police pound when Fred runs an errand. She stops the £28 recovery fee from his wages.

JUNE

Eddie acquires a metal detector, in the hope of finding buried treasure. Albert craftily tells him he has found coins on his allotment and Eddie, Stan and Hilda eagerly dig it over for him. Billy asks Deirdre to marry him and move to Jersey.

After second thoughts she declines.

Eddie takes a job selling ice-cream in the park, and enlists Stan's help. They sell beer out of the van to thirsty fathers, until the police warn them off.

JULY

Len is too busy to take a holiday, so Rita and Bet book a caravan in Morecambe. Bet picks up two men, and an uneasy Rita agrees to a caravan drinks party. The men sleep in the spare bunks, after losing their caravan keys, but Len arrives on the doorstep at breakfast time. The Faircloughs return to the Street at loggerheads.

Suzie Birchall starts at the factory, and inspires Hilda to apply for training as a machinist. Mike Baldwin tells her she is too old. Ken cooks Deirdre steak *au poivre*, ending with brandy and a growing understanding.

AUGUST

Gail calls on Ivy with her wedding present list, and the Tilsleys invite them to live at No. 5 when they are married. Betty Turpin's carriage clock is stolen by a mate of Eddie Yeats. She gives Eddie twenty-four hours to return it before she calls in the police.

Hilda buys a home piano tutor, but Annie refuses to let her near the Rovers piano. Hilda learns secretly on it when Annie is out, and plays *Beautiful Dreamer* to applause from Ena.

SEPTEMBER

On a quiet Sunday morning an electrical fault triggers the factory burglar alarm, and no-one has a key to turn it off. After seven disturbed hours, an irate Stan hits it with a poker and blacks out the whole Street. Mike Baldwin returns on Monday to find he has no power supply, and demands £200 damages from Stan.

Ken and Deirdre return from a short holiday in the Lake District, and joke about the stir they have caused. They retire to a candle-lit dinner at Ken's and kiss. Next day Deirdre receives a letter from Ray, and bursts into tears.

OCTOBER

Ray seeks a divorce and threatens to cite Ken as co-respondent. A nervous Ken tells Deirdre to keep him out of it, and she realizes he has no feelings for her.

Mavis Riley hears noises in the night and is convinced they are psychic phenomena. Eddie volunteers to keep watch, but falls asleep. The following night he hears them too, and cowers in Mavis' room for safety. It turns out to be a bird trapped behind the boarded-up fireplace.

NOVEMBER

A yellow budgie is found in Mavis' chimney by RSPCA man Harry Scott, who allows her to keep it. His mate Jack Walsh, forty and single, redecorates the room, and Mavis asks him to dinner. Ken Barlow tells Deirdre he needs her, and they kiss and make up.

Ron Mather returns from Torquay and asks Elsie to join him. She shocks Suzie by putting the house up for sale and leaving. Brian and Gail have a white wedding in church, with Ivy as matron of honour.

DECEMBER

Annie provides free champagne for the reception at the Rovers. Hilda is invited as washer-up. Suzie Birchall tries to safeguard her lodgings by putting off prospective house-buyers, but Elsie orders her out. Mike Baldwin catches her using his phone to ring her new punk boyfriend, and sacks her.

Five tickets are available for an exchange visit to Weatherfield's twin town in France. Hilda wins one, but learns that it will still cost her £60. She sells her 1950s clothes to a New Wave boutique to raise the money. Elsie is back from Torquay, and tells everyone she is staying for good.

JANUARY

Emily is upset that Dawson's has been taken over by Jim Sedgewick, who turns it into a transport cafe and installs a juke box. Unable to stand it any longer, she walks out and Elsie takes over as manageress. Rita walks out on Len after a blazing row about improving the house, and disappears. Hilda returns from the exchange visit to France to find that Stan has rented out the house as a love nest to Eddie and Fred and their girlfriends.

FEBRUARY

Ken tells Deirdre he won't risk a third marriage because he is too old, and Deirdre knows it is over. Mavis receives obscene phone calls, and the police persuade her to arrange a meeting with the man. As they lie in wait Eddie stops to chat to her and is leapt upon by officers.

Len finds Rita working in a Blackpool laundrette, but she refuses to return. The Ogdens have great expectations — Stan receives a solicitor's letter telling him that he is a beneficiary in a customer's will.

MARCH

Annie irks the Rovers staff by installing a bell to summon them. Fred chauffeurs Annie and her VIP guest, Olive Taylor-Brown, to a Ladies' Evening, but leaves her handbag containing the tickets on the car roof. Annie, humiliated, is refused admission.

Stan's legacy turns out to be £100 and a pot dog. Elsie, now into bed and breakfast, takes in a romeo lorry driver, and has to throw his bags into the Street. Mike Baldwin discovers that shop steward Ivy has not been democratically elected, and insists on a ballot.

APRIL

Ivy scrapes home with three votes over Ida Clough. Ena Sharples leaves for St Annes and appears for the last time. The Rovers enters a barbershop quartet competition. Organizer Fred Gee is thrown out for singing flat, and Renee is substituted, disguised as a man. The Flying Horse wins.

Brian and Gail go house-hunting and put down a deposit on a £16,000 plot. Hilda reads money in Stan's cup, and drags him to the bingo hall. They lose the jackpot – and Vera Duckworth wins a seaside holiday.

MAY

Gail and Brian have mortgage problems, until Ivy secretly gives them her £300 holiday savings. Rita returns to work permanently at the Kabin. Arnold Swain, a client at Emily's new typing agency, asks her for a date – her first since Ernest's death.

Stan is barred from the Rovers for arguing about bar prices. Annie lifts the ban when Ken defends his right to free speech. Bet throws out her new live-in lover, lorry driver Dan Johnson, for assaulting one of her flat neighbours in a fit of jealousy.

JUNE

Ivy Tilsley is promoted to factory supervisor. Pet shop owner Arnold Swain proposes to Emily, who turns him down, but wants to remain friends. Gail forgets to take the Pill and becomes pregnant. Eddie puts up a hanging basket for Mavis and brings the ceiling down. Mavis and her budgie have to move into Len's while repairs are done.

Renee thinks of selling the shop, and searches for a nice sub-post office in Grange-over-Sands. Ken runs a charity raffle. The prize – a date with a mysterious Mr Wonderful.

JULY

Hilda wins and finds out that her escort is Mike Baldwin, who offers her £40 to call it off. Alf and Renee sell the shop and celebrate at a country pub. Renee drives home, but stalls at traffic lights. As Alf jumps out to take over a lorry hits the car, flinging Renee through the windscreen. She dies in hospital, and Alf is breathalysed.

Elsie falls asleep and sets the armchair on fire, but Hilda arrives to borrow a cup of sugar and saves her life. Hilda basks in free brandy, milking every drop of glory, until Elsie explodes and their natural emnity resumes.

AUGUST

Emily changes her mind and agrees to a September wedding. Alf Roberts decides to keep the shop after Renee's funeral. Brian and Gail are pressured by a salesman to buy a new 'micro-bijou' house. Hilda is thrown out of the factory pools syndicate for not paying her dues. She takes the copy coupon from the sewing room noticeboard, and substitutes one with winning results.

SEPTEMBER

The elated factory girls, thinking they have won a fortune, discover that Hilda has conned them, and insist that Mike Baldwin sacks her. Arnold and Emily marry at Weatherfield Register Office.

Elsie's grandson, Martin Cheveski, runs into trouble with his girlfriend's father for getting her drunk. Bet loses her handbag in the sales at Marshall's store. A hoaxer rings to ask her to collect it and, when she is out, her flat is stripped by burglars.

OCTOBER

Rovers regulars raise £56 for Bet. Emily is worried by a belligerent change in Arnold's character. Martin and his girlfriend Karen defy her father's ban and continue dating. Brian is sacked from the garage for taking his mother-in-law out in a client's car. Fred Gee holds a birthday party while Annie is away, and scratches her sideboard. She insists that he pays for the French polishing.

NOVEMBER

When Eddie Yeats publicly discloses the contents of Annie's dustbin, she demands to have the refuse team changed. Weatherfield binmen boycott the Rovers. Stan is prevented from removing the rubbish in his handcart, and Fred from smuggling it out in the Rover. Annie has to climb down and apologize.

Len, tired of taunts from Rita on how the Yard is run, suggests they swop jobs. Rita takes over the Yard, and lands a substantial business deal. Stan develops an itching problem in the Rovers, and blames the rubbish.

DECEMBER

Stan is delivered a body blow – the doctor tells him he is allergic to beer. He climbs on the wagon a broken man, until the doctor diagnoses that eggs are to blame. A smirking Hilda informs Annie that she has taken on a charlady, Brenda Palin. Hilda sacks her when Annie offers Brenda a job at the Rovers.

Mike Baldwin's slippery father Frankie disappears to London with £70 Fred has invested in a video project. Arnold Swain, to Emily's horror, is exposed as a bigamist. He begs for another chance, but a distraught Emily sends him packing. Gail gives birth to a 7lb 2oz baby boy.

```

# 1981

## JANUARY

Gail secretly changes her baby's name from David Daniel to Nicholas Paul, to prevent his initials becoming DDT. Frankie Baldwin appears and repays Fred's money, but reveals that the Vice Squad are after him. The cheque bounces. Ken buys a Volkswagen Beetle, but Albert refuses to ride in a 'Jerry car'.

Ken and Deirdre rekindle their friendship, but she stands Ken up when a Dutch friend of Ray's arrives with a present for Tracey. Eddie and his mates enter the 'Cleanest Dustcart Competition'.

## FEBRUARY

Ken and Deirdre make up, but Mike Baldwin steps in to ask her on a date. Fred Gee tosses pie crusts onto the dustcart roof, attracting a flock of pigeons. Eddie and Co. wash off the dirt in time to tie for first prize.

Annie departs on a cruise, bringing in relief manager Gordon Lewis, a tough disciplinarian. He suspends Fred for drinking free Scotch, and accuses Betty of short-changing. Elsie makes a play for rugged trucker Wally Randle who eats at the cafe.

## MARCH

Ken takes beautician Sonia Price to Mike Baldwin's flat-warming party. Mike whisks her to a night-club, leaving Ken with Deirdre. Annie returns to find her staff gone and new barmaids installed. She restores everything to normal and sends an unflattering report on Lewis to the brewery.

Arnold Swain returns to terrorize Emily and is admitted to a mental home. Emily holidays in Malta with Mavis to recuperate. Annie invites Fred's presentable new ladyfriend Eunice Nuttall to supper, and dampens Fred's ardour by sending her home in a taxi. Hilda packs her washing for the laundrette in a bin liner, and the dustmen take it to the tip.

182
```

APRIL

Fred, promised his own pub when he marries, proposes to Eunice, and she accepts. Annie offers them a room at the Rovers for £10 a week. Ken has plans to marry Deirdre, but Brian and Gail's marriage hits a rocky patch. Elsie takes to the gin when Wally Randle rejects her advances. She realizes she is getting old. Elsie picks up roughneck Bill Fielding and takes him home for the night. When she goes to work, disgusted with herself, his jealous wife breaks in and slashes all Elsie's clothes.

MAY

Jack Duckworth turns Vera out because she has a boyfriend, Harry. Bert Tilsley begs him to take her back, but Jack is happier on his own. Vera returns after a bout of conscience. Fred and Eunice marry at Weatherfield Register Office. Albert, who expects to move in with Ken and Deirdre when they marry, is told they are thinking of moving away. When he is alone he quietly weeps. Colin Jackson, a friend of Gail and Brian, makes advances to Gail when Brian is out. She kicks him out, and Brian breaks off the friendship.

JUNE

Fred is turned down for his own pub – Eunice was sacked for stealing when she was a barmaid. Broody Rita wants to adopt a child. Len will not consider it, but they agree to foster. Ken and Deirdre book the wedding and ask a delighted Albert if they can move in with him. Emily and Mavis plan to go to London for the Royal Wedding.

JULY

Annie orders Fred and Eunice to leave, but relents when his replacement cannot take the job. Ken and Deirdre are married at All Saints Church and honeymoon in Corfu. Decorator Marcus Dodds starts work on the Rovers. He turns out to be an amateur artist, and persuades Mavis to pose nude for him. They both have second thoughts and call it off. Elsie is offered a machinist's job at the factory. Len and Rita, overjoyed, hear they have been selected to foster a thirteen-year-old.

AUGUST

Fred and Eunice move out of the Rovers into her father's flat. Len and Rita foster likeable John Spencer while his mother is in hospital. Brian has an affair with flirtatious garage customer Glenda Fox, and an angry Gail gives him a warning. Jack and Vera Duckworth celebrate their twenty-fourth wedding anniversary. Tracey gets chicken pox, and a worried Albert moves in with Emily in case he catches it.

SEPTEMBER

Albert is banned from the Ogden's as a 'domino-sharp', after beating them two nights in succession. Fred and Eunice move into the Community Centre as caretakers. Bet Lynch organizes the brewery's 'Mr and Mrs' competition, but Annie wonders if any Street marriages will stand up to it. Gail and Brian's victory is drowned in a row between all the other couples. Hilda gets a job cleaning Mike Baldwin's luxury flat. Mike's father Frankie is back, in the money, with a dazzling secretary on his arm. Brian Tilsley, working at a filling station, tackles a boy trying to rob the till, and puts him on the hospital critical list.

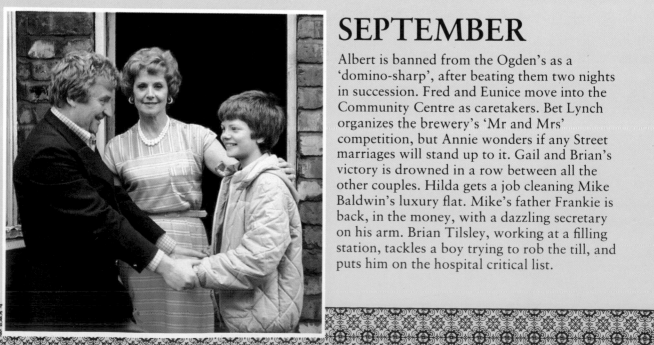

OCTOBER

Brian is arrested for unlawful wounding. Gail's mother Audrey, gives shampoo and sets in the back of the Corner Shop while Alf is away. Alf, completely smitten, turns a blind eye, and starts gossip by painting out Renee's name on the shop sign. Mike Baldwin, left with orders on his hands when a customer goes bankrupt, opens a market stall to clear the stock.

NOVEMBER

Vera deserts Ida and Ivy on the stall to help a rival stallholder who fancies her. Brian is cleared in court of the assault charge. Audrey Potter talks a besotted Alf into buying her a car. When he proposes she backs away quickly and goes back to her old boyfriend. Fred Gee is asked to leave the Centre because he is rude to the public.

DECEMBER

The councillor who sacks Fred, offers them jobs at his private hotel. Eunice accepts, but Fred refuses and goes back to the Rovers. Their marriage appears to be over. Emily receives news that Arnold Swain has died and left her £2,000. Annie, in her endless quest for sophistication, launches a Cocktail Hour at the Rovers.

JANUARY

Emily spends Arnold's legacy on a new trampoline for the youth club and a bed for the hospital. Arnold's penniless widow Margaret calls, and Emily gives her £2,000 of her own money. Ron Sykes, Brian's boss, is transferring the firm to the Persian Gulf, and Brian takes up his offer to work in Qatar. Annie is invited to the brewery's Bicentenary Ball. When her escort falls ill at the last minute, she is obliged to ask Fred. Betty is visited by her son Gordon and his fiancee Caroline Watson.

FEBRUARY

Annie counts the cost of Fred's drunken behaviour: a Space Invaders game and a new Rover are delivered – both ordered under the influence at the ball – followed by a barmaid who was promised a job. Stan forgets Hilda's birthday, despite her giving him the money to buy chocolates.

Ken tells Deirdre he does not want any more children. Eddie gets a CB radio and dates Stardust Lil, alias Marion Willis. He borrows the keys to Mike Baldwin's luxury flat from the Ogdens and entertains her. Gail makes friends with her new neighbour Jackie Moffatt, who takes her on a night out while Brian is away.

MARCH

The Faircloughs foster sixteen-year-old Sharon Gaskell, who turns out to be keen on soccer and good at woodwork. Fred Gee falls down the cellar steps, and considers suing Annie. She tells him that if his claim succeeds he will have to look for a lighter job, and Fred is soon back at work.

Gail rings Brian and finds that he is spending his leave in Cairo instead of Weatherfield. She decides to go out on the town. Betty Turpin's old lodger, travelling electrician Alec Hobson, moves back in with her.

APRIL

Bored Gail gets her old job back at the cafe, while neighbour Jackie baby-sits for her. Mavis' old flame Derek Wilton turns up with flowers. Mavis melts a little when he mentions a summer cruise, but sends him packing when he reveals he is taking his sister, not her.

Marion – Stardust Lil – wants to keep her past secret, and Eddie has difficulty expressing his feelings for her. Jack Duckworth fancies Bet and takes her to the Huntsman, where they narrowly miss bumping into Vera with her boyfriend. Vera finds out and dumps Jack's clothes at the Rovers.

MAY

Eddie tells Marion about his prison record and clumsily proposes. She accepts and they have a rowdy engagement party at the Rovers. Mike Baldwin discovers that his wages clerk has inadvertently given everyone a rise. He fires her and takes on Emily, who upsets the girls by deducting it from their wages.

Betty Turpin is mugged by a youngster from Ken's youth club. Deirdre quietly tips off the police, who thank her in front of Ken. Hilda wants a new three-piece suite, but the HP company turns her down as a bad credit risk. Binman Eddie is paid a fiver to dispose of an old suite, which he sells to Hilda as a 'modern antique'.

JUNE

Ken surprises Deirdre by suggesting they start a family of their own. Len and Rita take in Sharon for long-term fostering. Cleopatra, the factory cat, knocks coffee over the wage ledgers, and ruins Mike Baldwin's £50 sports-coat. He takes it to the RSPCA, but the girls retrieve it and make it a member of the union. Enthusiasm wanes when Mike includes the cat in the bonus share-out. There is panic when toddler Nicky Tilsley disappears. A big search of the Street finds him locked in Len's new house.

JULY

Elsie goes away and Eddie plans to spend the night with Marion. He tells Hilda that Elsie is ill in bed, and has to hide in the back yard when she calls to visit her. Mike Baldwin is comforted by his girlfriend Maggie Dunlop when his father dies. Their feelings grow, and he invites her to move in with him. Hilda, who cleans the flat, is shocked, so Mike gives her a £1 rise.

Brian Tilsley is home from the Gulf when Gail's admirer Les Charlton drops in. Brian makes a last minute decision not to go back. Len sells Chalkie Whiteley his old house, and the Fairclough's move into the new one.

AUGUST

Mavis' budgie Harry surprises her by laying an egg. She changes its name to Harriet, and warms the egg in her bra to see if it will hatch. Annie finds a lady's lighter in her Rover. Fred lent the car to a bookie to pay off gambling debts, and his wife asks worried Fred for her lighter back.

Brian Tilsley opens a garage in partnership with his boss Ron Sykes, and invests his £2,000 savings from Qatar. Len and Rita discover that Chalkie Whiteley's grandson Craig, living in their old house next door, plays the drums.

SEPTEMBER

Annie thinks Fred is having an affair with the bookie's wife. Mike Baldwin breaks up with his girlfriend Maggie. Eddie and Marion have called off the engagement, but Elsie and Hilda contrive to bring them together again. Hilda puts up a friend of Eddie, and finds that he is on the run. Sharon Gaskell meets Brian Tilsley for the first time and develops a crush on him.

1982

OCTOBER

Chalkie Whiteley's drumming grandson Craig decides to keep pigeons. When someone releases them, Len is suspected. Sharon volunteers to baby-sit for the Tilsleys, and Gail suggests that Brian drives her home. He is embarrassed when she kisses him goodnight, and more so when she gives him a zodiac key-ring for his birthday. Hilda gets a cleaning job for a Dr and Mrs Lowther and regales the Rovers with stories of their luxurious lifestyle.

NOVEMBER

Sharon breaks down when Brian tells her to stop chasing him. Mavis joins a literary class and meets Victor Pendlebury who asks her to collaborate on a short story. When it is read on local radio, Mavis worries in case it is too earthy: Annie Walker is disgusted – Albert thinks it is rubbish. Marion breaks off her engagement to Eddie when he loses their savings in a suspect car import business.

DECEMBER

Sharon is offered a kennelmaid's job in Sheffield, but Len and Rita hope she won't go. Marion launches a CB radio search for Eddie, and they have a loving reunion in Liverpool's dockland. Mike Baldwin threatens to sack Ivy when he discovers that the girls are making handbags on the side. Deirdre rows with Ken and spends a cosy evening at Mike's flat. Annie calls unexpectedly on the Ogdens and catches them trying on cast-off clothing from Hilda's employer. An incredulous Annie is convinced they privately dress for dinner. The Street throws a Christmas Cabaret, and Bet and Betty persuade Annie to hold a staff party.

JANUARY

Deirdre tells Ken she is visiting a girlfriend, but spends another cosy evening at Mike's flat. More dates follow as Ken breaks his promises to take her out. Eddie writes-off Annie's Rover by backing the bin lorry into it.

Handbag-Sammy Patel makes the factory girls another offer to manufacture bags on the quiet. Mike hears about the profit involved, and decides to make it legal. The girls refuse unless they get a bonus.

FEBRUARY

Suzie Birchall returns and Fred offers her the job of relief barmaid at the Rovers. Emily confronts Deirdre about her affair with Mike. He pressures Deirdre to leave Ken and marry him. Deirdre rows with Ken and confesses her affair. They sleep apart, but talk out their problems and decide to give it another try. Ken books a getaway holiday in Malta and warns Mike to stay off.

A disgruntled Annie learns that Fred has bought her wrecked Rover, and makes it clear she still expects to be chauffeured in it. Brian Tilsley removes the battery from Len's van until he pays a repair bill.

MARCH

Stan, realizing his window-cleaning days are over, is £185 in debt to moneylender Syd Kippax. Eddie buys the round and employs Stan, who finds him a tough boss. Bert Tilsley confides in Brian that he has had a slight stroke, but dare not tell Ivy. Brian takes out a bank loan and buys the garage business for himself. Fred Gee takes up with middle-aged Maureen Slater, who lives twenty miles away in Warrington. Whenever Fred gives her a lift home, she runs up the path, leaving him speechlessly unfulfilled. Hilda's well-to-do employers, Dr and Mrs Lowther, call with a message for her, and are momentarily taken aback to encounter Stan in his vest.

APRIL

Eddie helps Marion move into Elsie's front parlour and turn it in into a bed-sit. Mike, Len and Alf join forces to open a wine-bar disco. Despite loud opposition from the locals, plans for the Graffiti Club are passed. Mavis is forty-six, and Rita gives her a porcelain budgie, which she christens Bunty. Victor Pendlebury also arrives with a surprise. He has arranged a camping holiday in the Lake District, and brings a tent for them to practise. Elsie has a caller who tells her he is Suzie's husband. Elsie leaves them alone, and returns to find Suzie bruised and battered.

MAY

Fred Gee takes Bet and Betty to the park in his car, which rolls into the lake when he parks it. They arrive at the Rovers late and dishevelled to find chaos – Vera is helping behind the bar. Pam Mitchell of the *Weatherfield Recorder*, a local freesheet, asks Ken to write an advice column. Bet joins a video agency and is shown a tape of medallion-man Vince St Clair, who turns out to be Jack Duckworth. Bet persuades Vera to join as Carole Munro, and arranges a date between them at the Rovers. Mavis agonizes over an invitation from Victor to embark on a trial marriage.

JUNE

Mavis, still uncertain about the trial arrangement, visits Victor's cottage and is angry to learn that he has told his neighbour she is 'Mrs Pendlebury'. Hilda inherits a chip shop from her late brother Archie. She decides to sell it after a wrangle with Archie's common law wife, and invests the profit in new carpets and a bidet. Deirdre is beginning to worry about *Recorder* editor Pam Mitchell's influence over Ken.

JULY

Bet Lynch launches a slimming contest at the Rovers. Fred is disqualified for cheating by filling his pockets with loose change and discarding it for the final weigh-in. Mike Baldwin meets a Russian trade delegation and dates the interpreter. Bert, helping at the garage while Brian gives Gail a driving lesson, causes an explosion by overinflating a tyre. Ivy silently prays as he lies unconscious in hospital.

AUGUST

Chalkie Whiteley emigrates to Australia, and the Street has reservations as the Duckworths buy his house for £10,000. Bert Tilsley, discharged from hospital, is missing. Police trace him to Bristol, where he is suffering from a mental breakdown. Ken is summoned to the Town Hall after leaking a plan to close youth clubs to the *Recorder*. He refuses to sign a loyalty agreement, and takes voluntary redundancy. Percy Sugden is appointed Centre caretaker.

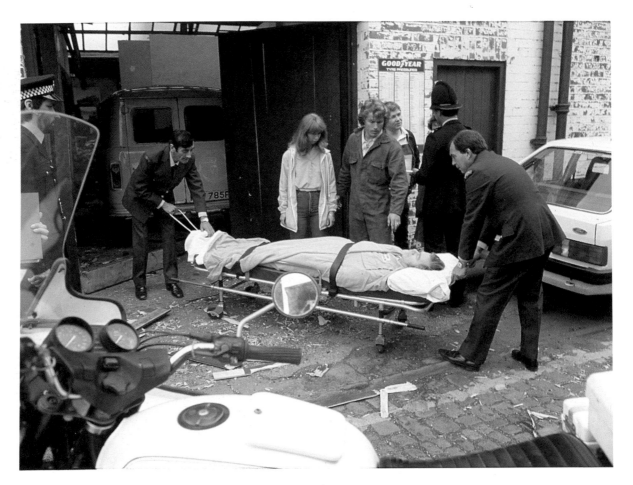

SEPTEMBER

Opening night at the Graffiti Club: half the Street are refused admission to the ticket-only night. A huge row erupts in the foyer while Hilda, the cloakroom attendant, looks smugly on. The Duckworths move their furniture into Chalkie's empty house to avoid storage charges. A violent struggle ensues with auctioneers who empty the house to take the furniture to a saleroom. Gail fails her driving test, and Brian puts the ailing garage up for sale. Hilda opens a bank account with the remains of her legacy and takes Stan out for a high-class meal. Terry Duckworth challenges Fred to prove he was a Para. Fred jumps from a back-yard wall and lands on a dustbin, hurting his back.

OCTOBER

Gail and Brian sell their 'micro-bijou' home and move in with Ivy. Betty objects to the Rovers new staff uniforms, which look like spray-on T-shirts. Marion and Eddie decide to marry as she is expecting a baby. The news leaks out and Fred taunts Eddie. They fight and Eddie arrives at church with a black eye. The best man is late because Jack Duckworth's taxi breaks down. The Street Autumn Fayre ends in acrimony when the Deputy Mayoress chooses Hilda's cake instead of Annie's. Ken tells a shocked Deirdre that he has sunk his redundancy money into a partnership in the *Weatherfield Recorder*.

NOVEMBER

Annie retreats from Eddie and Marion's wedding reception when the best man reads out suggestive telegrams. Emily Bishop takes in binman Curly Watts as a lodger. Ken writes a crusading article attacking the Graffiti Club. Fearing loss of advertising, his partner orders him to rewrite it as a flattering piece. Ken reluctantly complies, describing Mike Baldwin as 'the debonaire dynamo of denim'. Hilda wants to go abroad to celebrate her Ruby Wedding. They apply for a duplicate birth certificate for Stan's passport, and find that he is sixty-four, not sixty-one. Percy Sugden introduces his gentleman budgie, Randy, to Mavis' Harriet. She is horrified and accuses Randy of being rough and uncouth. Percy takes him home in a huff.

DECEMBER

Hilda and Stan book the Rovers for their Ruby Wedding. Eddie and Marion say goodbye before leaving for a new life in Bury, and Rita has just sung *Stardust* when the news comes through that Len has been killed in a motorway crash. After the funeral Rita finds that Len died on his way back from meeting another woman.

JANUARY

Elsie Tanner appears for the last time. Her old flame Bill Gregory takes her for a night out and asks her to go back to Portugal with him. At the last moment Elsie rings his London hotel and says she is on her way. When the taxi-driver asks her how long she will be gone, Elsie gives a Mona Lisa smile and replies: 'Now there's a question.'

Stan injures his foot on a broken paving stone and decides to sue the council. Ken backs his claim by publishing a close-up of Stan's big toe in the *Recorder*. Ivy is summoned to hospital to find that Bert has died. Mike Baldwin sells his share in the Graffiti Club when he finds that the books are being fiddled.

FEBRUARY

Stan accepts £200 compensation from the council. Percy draws the winning ticket when Fred raffles his Rover. Fred is incensed when Kevin Webster buys it for banger-racing. Kevin's father Bill rents Len's old yard from Rita and sets up as a repairman. Annie, who is absent, telephones the Rovers and tells a horrified Bet and Betty that she is putting Fred in charge as temporary manager. On his first day Fred tries to increase business by buying pies. He eats one and becomes violently ill.

MARCH

Hilda receives her first bank statement and is livid to find that Stan has withdrawn £40 without telling her. Kevin Webster agrees to give Mavis driving lessons for £2 an hour, but gives it up as 'suicidal'. Belligerent Billy Walker comes home to run the Rovers while Fred is in hospital, and offends everyone. Bill Webster borrows £1,000 from Rita to finance his property repair business and makes Alf jealous. Emily finds out that Bill is known to the police and has his job repairing the Chapel roof cancelled. Ivy upsets admirer Arthur Whitaker as she is not ready for a serious relationship yet.

APRIL

The Rovers stand-in manager Frank Harvey invites Bet to a brewery dance when the new barmaid turns him down. Bet turns up dressed as a tramp to strike a blow for Women's Lib. Curly Watts is depressed at his lack of success with girls, and organizes a canal cruise. Ken becomes entangled with the problems of one of his advice column clients. The TV detector van calls at the Duckworth's. Jack admits that they have no licence, and is relieved to find that Vera is responsible because it is in her name.

MAY

Alf Roberts, on the campaign trial, is re-elected to the council. Gail and Brian make up a foursome with friends for a night out at a casino. Gail is upset when Brian loses money at the tables. Relief manager Gordon Lewis takes over the Rovers and introduces a disciplinary regime. Albert Tatlock's daughter Beattie arrives with news that Albert has died. She gives Ken her father's Military Medal after the funeral. Billy Walker is back at the Rovers. He finds life dull and starts a poker school and pesters Deirdre. The Duckworths are fined £150 for the TV offence, instead of the £250 they expected. They get drunk to celebrate, and Jack falls over the TV set, smashing it.

JUNE

Mavis passes her driving test and, after a celebratory drink, reverses into Jack Duckworth's taxi. Bill Webster buys Elsie's house, but has trouble persuading Elsie's daughter, Linda Cheveski, to move out. Amateur astronomer Curly Watts sights a UFO and is interviewed on Radio Weatherfield. Billy Walker's sophisticated girlfriend Samantha Benson turns up from Jersey to tell him that his creditors are waiting for their cash.

JULY

The Rovers Return takes on the Flying Horse in the Pub Olympics. Hilda wins the egg and spoon race after Vera is disqualified for pushing. At the ensuing Talent Contest, Vera and Ivy sing *We're a Couple of Swells*, and Billy Walker asks Emily to lend him £6,000. When a solicitor appears, bearing a final demand, Billy leaves to ask Annie for money. Betty, looking after the Rovers in his absence, hears a noise in the night. She turns on the light to find the front door ajar, and a half-consumed pint of beer gently quivering on the bar.

AUGUST

Derek Wilton takes Mavis for an Italian meal and swears he will prove just how much he has changed. They become engaged, but Mavis' old flame Victor gatecrashes the party to announce that he has not given up the fight for her hand. Billy Walker returns and tells the staff that he is taking over the Rovers. He goads Fred into punching him on the jaw so that he can fire him. Gail, against Brian and Ivy's advice, takes over the cafe when the manageress retires. Percy Sugden loses Randy, his budgie, and offers £10 reward. Jack Duckworth buys a budgie for £2, and tries to con him, but Percy has already found his pet.

SEPTEMBER

When the Corner Shop is robbed, Percy organizes a citizens' home-watch, and is arrested as a suspected peeping tom. Victor has conceded defeat, and Mavis' wedding day arrives. Mavis realizes she cannot marry Derek, and that she never really loved him. Rita tells the vicar, and bumps into the best man who is delivering an identical message from Derek. Ken appears jealous when his *Recorder* assistant Sally Waterman stays the night at the Rovers with Billy Walker.

OCTOBER

Mavis is insulted that Derek did not turn up for the wedding – and prepares to face people. Ken falls in love with *Recorder* reporter Sally Waterman, who is dating Billy Walker, but both Billy and Deirdre are suspicious.

Jack Duckworth, breathalysed after celebrating Vera's £250 bingo win, is banned for a year and fined £200. He loses his job taxi-driving, but the future looks inviting on the dole – until he learns he cannot claim benefit. Jack sells shirts on the market. Betty Turpin takes in a police lodger, Sergeant Tony Cunliffe, who makes an arresting impression on Bet Lynch. Brian Tilsley throws out his mother-in-law's lover, George Hepworth, after discovering he made a pass at Gail. There is friction when Brian thinks Gail has not told him just how far George went.

NOVEMBER

Fred Gee poses as Mike Baldwin to sell shirts with Jack. They collect a £400 cheque – made out to Mike. He agrees to cash it, deducting 30 per cent for income tax. Tony Cunliffe breaks with Bet and sets his sights on a reluctant Rita. Hilda collapses from the strain of nursing sick Stan, and the doctor sends him to hospital. Police raid a Rovers late drinks session.

Hilda is shattered by a phone call telling her Stan is dead. The grave's headstone, on her instructions, has space for two names. Hilda weeps over the parcel of Stan's belongings sent from the hospital. Fred Gee, working at Baldwins, is given the sack and leaves the Street.

DECEMBER

Vera buys Stan's window-cleaning round for £100 and sends Jack, complaining, out to work. He enjoys the job when he meets friendly Dulcie Froggart, but Vera thinks he is exhausted through overwork. Billy Walker, carpeted by the brewery, gives up the tenancy, and leaves the Street for Jersey. Newton & Ridley advertise for a manager for the Rovers – Bet, Jack Duckworth and temporary manager Gordon Lewis all apply.

Despite Percy Sugden's protestations, romance blossoms between his niece, Elaine Prior, and Bill Webster. They plan to marry and move to Southampton, but Kevin Webster is upset and refuses to go. Rita and Tony end their relationship when he realizes she cannot get over Len's death.

JANUARY

Brewery chief Sarah Ridley offers Gordon another pub and Bet the Rovers. Hilda takes a paying guest – Henry Wakefield, who later confesses he is out of work after being blacked for strike-breaking at a local foundry. Hilda insists he stays and persuades Mike Baldwin to give him a job.

Kevin Webster turns up at the last minute for the wedding, and makes friends with his father. Bill offers to let him live at the house until it is sold. Pushy designer Christine Millward sells her designs to Mike Baldwin. They make a successful business trip to London, and occupy separate hotel bedrooms, but they are clearly attracted to each other.

FEBRUARY

Mike Baldwin has high hopes for designer Christine Millward – until her husband David turns up. Old soldier Percy Sugden works hard organizing a charity Valentine's Dance at the Community Centre, then discovers, thunderstruck, that the DJ, 'Kaiser Bill', wears a German helmet. Bet Lynch, now with her name over the Rovers' door, finds running a pub hard work for a woman: then a stranger called Wilf Starkey walks in and offers his services.

MARCH

Andrea Clayton, with poor results in her mock A-levels, wants to leave school, but Ken Barlow persuades her to stay on. George Wardle, the new factory van driver, has an eye for Ivy Tilsley. He manages the church football team and talks her into washing their kit.

The story of Mavis' 'honeymoon that never was' attracts the Press. Angry Derek Wilton demands an explanation and threatens to sue the reporter. Ken gets into D.I.Y. difficulties. He goes out for help, and returns to find that Deirdre has finished the bookcase herself. Trouble at the Tilsley's – Gail wants a home of her own away from Ivy, but Brian prefers life the way it is. Meanwhile, at the Rovers, Bet has a visit from snooty Stella Rigby of the White Swan.

APRIL

Rovers regulars take on the White Swan in the Brainiest Pub Contest. It's neck and neck – until Percy Sugden lets them down on a football question, and they lose by one point. Bet tries not to choke on the defeat. Terry Duckworth and Curly Watts buy Jack's car and, with Kevin as mechanic, open a moonlighting business.

Gail walks out on Brian, taking Nicky with her, and rents a tatty bed-sit. After a row they are reconciled and agree to apply for a council house. Jack gives Vera a length of silver lurex to have a dress made up by Connie Clayton. Vera says she will make Joan Collins look like a lollipop lady. Jack's view: 'Don't ask me, kiddo. I'm only the husband.'

MAY

A bitter feud erupts between the Duckworths and the Claytons when Vera refuses to pay the £38 dress bill. Tight-fisted Terry agrees to settle it when the row threatens to cloud his love-life with Andrea. George Wardle invites Ivy to the church football semi-final. When the mini-bus breaks down they borrow Mike Baldwin's van without telling him. The opposing team daubs it with slogans, and a furious Mike threatens to sack them both. Only the intervention of a big order for jeans cools his temper, and he lets them off.

Kevin Webster, on a double date with Andrea and Terry, falls in love with uppercrust Michelle Robinson, from the 'better part' of Weatherfield. When her wealthy parents find out, Kevin finds himself battling against class barriers.

JUNE

Mike Baldwin wines and dines businessman Don Ashton to clinch a deal. Ashton leaves a briefcase containing £4000 in a nightclub loo, and is tragically killed on his way home. Hilda finds the case, but it is empty. Barman Wilf Starkey confesses to Bet that he took it, but Mike decides to keep it quiet because the deal was shady. Bet Lynch wants to sack Wilf, but Mike intervenes.

Bet, Rita and Mavis let their hair down on a holiday in Blackpool. They are all picked up by holiday romeos – but Mavis gets the only one who is not married.

JULY

Ivy and George take a holiday together. When they return he proposes and Ivy accepts. The Claytons, still fuming after their row with the Duckworths over Vera's dress, receive a shock – Andrea confesses that she is three month's pregnant, and Terry is the father.

Alf Roberts, planning to expand his shop, offers next-door-neighbour Hilda Ogden £15,000 for her house. She begins to hedge when she hears about the redevelopment scheme. Then Alf discovers that Mike Baldwin has been secretly advising Hilda on how to handle the sale.

AUGUST

Ivy and George marry with no complications, well, only a few. The rest of the Street have their own private recollections of former neighbours and friends – Annie Walker celebrating her seventy-sixth birthday quietly in Derby; Ken with thoughts of his first wife Val, who was electrocuted – they would have been together twenty-three years. Widow Emily Bishop's late husband Ernest would have been fifty-five on the 21st. Over in Bury, binman Eddie Yeats is probably celebrating his forty-fourth birthday with a knees-up.

SEPTEMBER

Age shall not weary them: Vera Duckworth is forty-nine. And in September 1968, Elsie Tanner was widowed when her GI husband Steve was found dead at the foot of the stairs. Victor Pendlebury ponders how different his forty-eighth birthday might have been with Mavis.

Life in the Street goes on – births, deaths, new faces and familiar friends. The world in another twenty-five years might be very different, but down Weatherfield way they will be sharing the same fun, tears, hopes and fears as the rest of us.

Twenty-five things you never knew about Coronation Street

1 Since the series began 20,720 pints have been drunk in the Rovers Return – a third of them, it was rumoured, by Stan Ogden.

2 *Coronation Street* was originally to be called 'Florizel Street'. The producers had a last minute change of mind when they thought it sounded like a brand of disinfectant.

3 Ken Barlow had the first indoor lavatory in the Street. It was installed at Number 9 in 1962.

4 Fifteen clergymen have been portrayed in the Street, but only one was real – The Rev Frank Topping who married Deirdre and Ken in 1981. 'Does that mean they are really married?' he was asked. 'Of course,' he replied, 'but only as Deirdre and Ken.'

5 The famous signature tune has been changed only once – it was jazzed-up by Steve Race for Emily Nugent's wedding in 1972.

6 Actor Bryan Mosley, better known as Alf Roberts, is an expert stunt man and a founder of the Society of British Fight Arrangers. Twice a year he presents his own award for stage fencing at RADA.

7 Animals featured in the Street over the past twenty-five years have included two chimpanzees, a monkey named Marlon, two whippets, four greyhounds, a pair of sea-lions, a boa constrictor, eleven pigeons, one newt, two budgies, a rabbit called Fred, a mongrel dog, two cats, six hens, a donkey, one labrador puppy and a mynah bird named Kitchener.

8 Since the factory opened in 1976 the sewing-room girls have bought more than 9000 balm cakes from the Corner Shop.

9 For twenty years, before the new set was built, the Gents lavatory door in the Rovers Return led into Albert Tatlock's kitchen.

10 Bernard Youens, who played Stan Ogden, narrowly missed being given the part of Jack Walker, landlord of the Rovers.

11 *Coronation Street* has been seen in eighteen countries, mostly with subtitles beneath – except in Hong Kong where Mandarin Chinese characters are displayed down the left-hand side.

12 Ena Sharples never wore a wedding ring because she had to have it cut off her finger when it became too tight in 1941. She could never afford another.

13 William Roache, who plays Ken Barlow, lived as an Arab among Bedouin tribesmen during his army career, and rode a camel.

14 Hilda Ogden's favourite drink is Planter's Punch – she gained a taste for it when working as a cleaner on a cruise ship.

15 There are Coronation Street Appreciation Societies at several British universities, including Cambridge.

16 Betty Turpin looks at home behind the Rovers Return bar because Betty Driver, who plays her, used to run her own country pub in Cheshire.

17 There have been twenty-three deaths, eight births and nineteen marriages in the Street since the series began.

18 The hardest *Coronation Street* costumes to buy are Hilda Ogden's flower-pattern pinafores. They cost only £3 on market stalls, but are so out of date they are difficult to find.

19 Little Warren Jackson, who plays Nicky Tilsley, was cast for the part before he was born. His parents, Jesmond and Peter Jackson, who are friends of Chris Quinten (Brian Tilsley) were expecting a baby at the same time as Gail. As both Nicky's parents are blond – like Brian and Gail – the chances were that the baby would be suitable. Warren arrived on 24 November 1980, and was twenty-one days old when he made his TV debut.

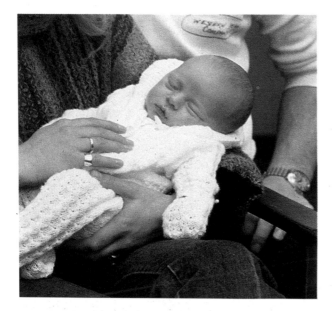

20 Johnny Briggs, who plays Mike Baldwin, had his first professional engagement on Boxing Night 1947, when he sang in *La Boheme* at the Cambridge Theatre as a boy soprano.

21 Julie Goodyear, better known as Bet Lynch, has received so many earrings from fans that she would have to wear a different pair every episode for thirty-five years to get through them all.

22 Actor Bill Waddington, who plays Percy Sugden, started in showbusiness more than forty years ago in 'The Blue Pencils', the first concert party recruited from the armed forces at the start of World War II.

23 Three members of the *Coronation Street* cast have been honoured by the Queen. Violet Carson (Ena Sharples) was awarded the OBE in 1965, Doris Speed (Annie Walker) the MBE in 1977, and Jack Howarth (Albert Tatlock) the MBE in 1983.

24 Those plaster ducks winging across Hilda Ogden's 'muriel' were first seen above Elsie Tanner's mantelpiece when the Street started.

25 For seven months in 1961 only thirteen contract actors were featured in *Coronation Street*. The rest of the cast were prevented from appearing by a national Equity strike. To keep the series running they were heard offstage, slamming doors and walking up and down stairs.

Nicholas Tilsley

The Street's forgotten stars

Hundreds of actors have walked down Coronation Street since 1960. While the main characters have become household names, others in cameo roles were often at the beginning of their careers. How many of these famous faces do you remember from early episodes?

This cheeky charmer is snake-dancer Eunice 'La Composita' Bond, Dennis Tanner's girlfriend, better known as Angela Douglas, wife of the late Kenneth More.

Comedy actor Bill Maynard does a passable impersonation of a lavatory brush . . . Bill appeared as song agent Micky Malone when Stan was stealing Ena's tunes and selling them.

This little Monkee is David Jones who played Ena's grandson, Colin Lomax, back in 1961. After giving him a biscuit Ena sent him on an errand to buy a form for her will. David only appeared in one episode . . . perhaps it was the haircut.

Prunella Scales appeared in the Street in 1961 as bus conductress Eileen Hughes – before she married Basil and moved to Fawlty Towers.

Still unmistakable – Joanna Lumley appeared in July 1973 as graduate Elaine Perkins, who caught Ken Barlow's roving eye.

Smooth-talking Ron Jenkins, alias actor Ben Kingsley, once chatted-up Irma Barlow in the Corner Shop – would Gandhi have approved?

Back in 1961 Jack Smethurst, as Fred Clark the bouncer at the Orinoco Club, complimented Elsie on her egg and chips.

Mollie Sugden, star of *That's My Boy* and *Are You Being Served?* popped up from time to time to score social points over Annie as Nellie Harvey of the Lady Licensed Victuallers.

Comedian Stan Stennett played Hilda Ogden's brother, chip-shop owner Norman Crabtree, but Stan Ogden thought there was something fishy about him.

Believe it or not, the double-chin and beads belong to today's lean, good-looking Martin Shaw, of *The Professionals*. In 1968 he played hippie commune leader Robert Croft who took over an empty house in the Street.

Angela Pleasance appeared as Monica Sutton, one of the Street's hippy commune. Monica's sister, Cockney Jenny Sutton, married Dennis Tanner.

Sir Julius Berlin, owner of the Warehouse and Ken Barlow's boss for a while, was played by Leonard Sachs, compère of the *Good Old Days*.

Comedian Max Wall made an appearance in the Street as Oldham-exile Harry Payne, who bumped into Elsie in Majorca.

'Ello, 'ello, can that be Richard
Beckinsale on the left, fearlessly
apprehending Ena Sharples? Richard
gave an arresting performance as PC
Wilcox of Tile Street Police Station in
April 1969.

George who? Patrick Troughton
played George Barton, father of union
organizer Peggy Barton, before he
became better known as Dr Who.

The Duke of Bedford, of course,
played himself when the Street
organized a coach trip to Woburn.
Only the aristocracy could bring Ena
to the brink of a smile.

Singer Peter Noone, of
Herman's Hermits, made a
brief appearance as Len
Fairclough's son Stanley.

209

Just how Street wise are you?

How much of *Coronation Street* do *you* remember over the past twenty-five years? Test your knowledge with these 100 teasers, guaranteed to bring back a flood of memories.

1 What was Eddie Yeats' CB radio handle?
   a) Harry Lime?
   b) Long John Silver?
   c) Slim Jim?

2 Who adopted a pigeon called Gilbert which was eaten by Minnie Caldwell's cat Bobby?

3 Len and Rita Fairclough were married on 20 April 1977. Who was Len's best man?

4 Annie Walker once tried to boost trade at the Rovers with a new gimmick. Hilda described it as: 'Like having tea in a dog kennel.' What was it?

5 Who left the Street by taxi in January 1984 to look after a bar in Portugal?
   a) Bet Lynch?
   b) Elsie Tanner?
   c) Marion Willis?

6 Which is the only house in Coronation Street without a telephone?

7 Who confessed to killing Steve Tanner and then shot himself?

8 Who had a Chinese girlfriend named Jasmine Chong?

9 Who passed her driving test in 1965 and has not driven since?

10 Mike Baldwin once threatened to get rid of the factory cat. How did the girls stop him?

11 In 1982 Mavis Riley's budgie caused some excitement. What happened?
   a) It escaped?
   b) It laid an egg?
   c) It learned to swear?

12 What make of car did Annie Walker buy after passing her driving test?

13 Soon after Len married Rita he was found unconscious while doing a plumbing job at Baldwin's factory. A heart attack was suspected – but what did the doctor diagnose?

14 Who moved into the Rovers as a pot-man after his wife had died in a warehouse fire?

15 In January 1982 Emily Bishop received a £2,000 legacy – from whom?

16 Albert Tatlock was once curator of his regimental museum. What was his old regiment?

17 In 1982 who proposed to the owner of the local florists, 'Maggie's Flowers', and was turned down?
   a) Ken Barlow?
   b) Eddie Yeats?
   c) Mike Baldwin?

18 Who regards herself as clairvoyant, and reads tea-leaves?

19 Who built a dinghy called *Shangri-la* in Len Fairclough's back yard?

20 Which Street resident was fined £2 for shoplifting in 1966?

21 In which year did Jack Walker die?
   a) 1970?
   b) 1974?
   c) 1978?

22 On the day of Elsie Tanner's wedding in 1967, who died under Len Fairclough's van when the jack collapsed?

23 Everyone in the Street was evacuated to the Glad Tidings Mission in 1971 – why?

24 Actress Angela Douglas, wife of the late Kenneth More, once played the part of a snake-charming stripper, who was Dennis Tanner's girlfriend. What was she called?

25 Who was the character who did not live in the Street, but deputized as Mission caretaker when Ena Sharples sprained her ankle?

26 Who was the actor who played Jack Walker?

27 In Coronation Street's 1976 pantomime Rita sang *When I Fall In Love* in the wings while Bet Lynch mimed on stage. Who did Len play?

28 When Alf Roberts became Mayor in 1973, who was his Mayoress?

29 On Hilda Ogden's sixtieth birthday in February 1984 the council awarded Stan compensation for stubbing his toe on a paving stone. How much did he get?
   a) £200?
   b) £400?
   c) £1,000?

30 The first words ever spoken in the Street were: 'Now the next thing you want to do is get a signwriter in.' Elsie Lappin said them – to whom?

31 Elsie Tanner's daughter had the first baby born in the series. What was her christian name – and what was the baby christened?

32 Ena Sharples played the organ for a wedding at the local Congregational Church on Easter Monday 1979 . . . Who was married?

33 The first death in the Street was a woman whose daughter accused her of malingering. Who was she?

34 Ken Barlow's father Frank appeared in the first episode. What was his job?

35 In 1964 Annie suspected Jack of infidelity, and left him when she found he had been sending money to a Mrs Nicholls. What was the innocent explanation?

36 Ken Barlow was a school teacher. What was the name of his school?

37 When Coronation Street's amateur dramatic society performed *The Importance of Being Ernest* in 1974, what part did Annie play?

38 In a tiff before they were married Rita pushed Len off a bar stool, and he hit his head. When she discovered that he was pretending the injury was worse than it was, what did she do?

39 To whom did Billy Walker sell his garage in 1972?

40 In September 1982 the Ogdens took in a friend of Eddie who was on the run from the police. What was his name?
   a) Harry Hewitt?
   b) Billy Nelson?
   c) Charlie Moffitt?

41 Who was the founder of the Private Property Owners and Small Traders Party in 1962?

42 Coronation Street's first wedding was in March 1961. The groom was Gordon Davies – who was the bride?

43 Eddie Yeats went into the guard dog business with a tatty alsatian called Fury. What happened to it?

44 In 1981 a garage thief accused a Street resident's son of unlawful wounding. Whom did he accuse?

45 What is the name of the brewery which supplies the Rovers Return?

46 In January 1968 a famous Street landmark was demolished. What was it, and who kept it clean?

47 In episode 2000, transmitted in June 1980, what was the Tilsley's good news?
   a) A mortgage?
   b) Brian's promotion?
   c) Gail's pregnancy?

48 Who fostered two black children, Vernon and Lucy Foyle, in 1974?

49 Where did widower Harry Hewitt propose to Concepta Riley, the Rovers Irish barmaid?

50 Alf Roberts was disabled for a fortnight after a fall in March 1983. What did he trip over?
   a) Bet Lynch's tights?
   b) Bet's handbag?
   c) Bet's shoe?

51 Elsie Tanner accepted a lift home from a gentleman in a country pub . . . What were the consequences?

52 In 1976 Bet Lynch gave away an old coat in the Rovers for a Bonfire Guy. To whom did it belong?

53 Emily Nugent had a shop in 1961 which she closed and merged with Leonard Swindley's. What did she sell?

54 Annie Walker bought a daffodil-gold outfit for her son Billy's wedding to Deirdre Hunt in 1975. To her dismay another woman bought an identical outfit – who was it?

55 In April 1983 Mavis Riley's boyfriend Victor Pendlebury gave her a birthday surprise. Was it:
   a) A day's potholing?
   b) A trip to the Blue John Mines?
   c) A camping holiday?

56 Who was the betting shop owner that Rita jilted in 1975 to marry Len?

57 Who was the burglar for whom Eddie Yeats 'cased' houses on his window-cleaning round?

58 Who died after being shot by two thugs in a wage snatch?

59 Gordon was always believed to be the son of Maggie Clegg at the Corner Shop. Who was his real mother?

60 Students held Annie Walker for a £5 ransom in a rag stunt – who paid it?

61 Ken Barlow's first marriage was in 1961. What was the maiden name of the girl he married?

62 On what religious grounds did Ivy Tilsley object to her son Brian marrying Gail Potter?

63 Who played the part of Britannia when the Street celebrated the Royal Jubilee in 1977?

64 What was the name of the relief barmaid Fred Gee engaged at the Rovers when he took over in April 1984?
    a) Nelly Howell?
    b) Kath Goodwin?
    c) Doreen Lostock?

65 Who bought the entire stock of Corner Shop candles and sold them in an electricity blackout?

66 When Ena Sharples collapsed with a slight stroke in 1961, she was visited by her daughter. What was her name?

67 How did Ken Barlow's mother Ida die in September 1961?

68 What kind of business did Leo and Mario Bonarti open in Rosamund Street in 1961?

69 How did Annie decorate the Rovers to win the 'Perfect Landlady Competition' in 1969?

70 Why did Len hand over the deeds to the Kabin to Rita in 1973?

71 Who was electrocuted while using a hairdryer with a faulty plug in 1971?

72 Eddie Yeats disappeared in 1982 after losing the money he had saved to get married. Where did Marion find him?
    a) London?
    b) The Flying Horse?
    c) Liverpool?

73 One of Albert Tatlock's often-told stories was about a certain pillar of the community who took part in the Co-op Pageant of 1933 as Lady Godiva, dressed only in a body stocking. Who on earth was he talking about?

74 Stan Ogden found himself in financial trouble in 1983 and went to a local moneylender. What was his name?
    a) Sharkey Heslop?
    b) Syd Kippax?
    c) Uncle Charlie?

75 What was the exact date and time of the first *Coronation Street* transmission?

76 Fred Gee, Alf Roberts and Terry Bradshaw bought a greyhound which they kept in the Rovers cellar. What was its name?

77 On Spring Bank Holiday 1984 Terry Duckworth, Kevin Webster and Curly Watts took their girlfriends out on a borrowed cabin cruiser. When the engine broke down, which couple stayed the night?
    a) Kevin and Mandy Whitworth?
    b) Terry and Gill Collins?
    c) Curly and Elaine Pollard?

78 Albert Tatlock proudly wore one of his wartime medals at a Street party for his eightieth birthday. Which was it?

79 When Rita resumed her club singing career in 1975 who became her pianist – despite his wife's disapproval?

80 For whom did Len Fairclough's first wife leave him in 1962?

81 Who wrestled Ian Campbell at the Viaduct Sporting Club in 1964?

82 When Mavis was ill with 'flu in 1984, who caught a trouserless man in her flat?

83 On what charge did Vera Duckworth once appear in court?
    a) Non-payment of rates?
    b) Shoplifting?
    c) No TV licence?

84 Back in 1963 Dennis Tanner launched window cleaner Walter Potts on a singing career. What was his stage name?

85 Who won the Premium Bonds in 1964 and moved from the Street?

86 Why was Len Fairclough late for his own wedding?

87 Someone in the Street had a romance with Hungarian building site worker Miklos Zadic. Who was she?

88 Billy Walker left the army in the opening months of the serial. What was his first job?

89 The police arrived when the burglar alarm was accidentally set off at Mike Baldwin's factory. Who was the culprit?

90 Len Fairclough built a house on the site of one which had collapsed in 1964. Who were the previous occupants?

91 Angry Ena quit the Mission in 1961 and moved in with Minnie, after being accused of something by Leonard Swindley. What was it?

92 Who was the eleven-year-old girl who ran away from an orphanage in 1961 to be near her father?

93 What was Alf Roberts job before he ran the Corner Shop?

94 The Street went to Blackpool Illuminations in 1961. Who was left behind by the coach and had to hitch-hike home on a lorry?

95 Before becoming engaged to his first wife Ken Barlow had an affair with Marion Lund. What was her job?

96 When the Rovers was evacuated because of a warehouse fire in 1975, Annie Walker lost a leather bag. What was in it?

97 What was the name of the warship on which both Len and Alan Howard served in World War II?

98 In the first episode of *Coronation Street* a customer asked the new owner of the Corner Shop for 'Half a dozen (fancies) – and no eclairs!' Who was she?

99 Ken Barlow resigned from his first job after a clash with his employers. What was the name of the firm?

100 Coronation Street once had its own night-club. What was it called?

ANSWERS

1 (c) Slim Jim. 2 Albert Tatlock. 3 Alf Roberts. 4 A Cocktail Hour. 5 (b) Elsie Tanner. 6 Hilda Ogden's. 7 Joe Donnelli. 8 Billy Walker. 9 Emily Bishop. 10 They made the cat a member of their union. 11 (b) It laid an egg. 12 Secondhand Rover 2000. 13 Overwork. 14 Fred Gee. 15 Her bigamous husband Arnold Swain who died in December 1981. 16 Lancashire Fusiliers. 17 (c) Mike Baldwin. 18 Hilda Ogden. 19 Jerry Booth. 20 Ena Sharples. 21 (a) 1970. 22 Harry Hewitt. 23 A fractured gas main caused the fear of an explosion. 24 Eunice Bond, known as 'La Composita'. 25 Martha Longhurst.

26 Arthur Leslie. 27 Buttons. 28 Annie Walker. 29 (a) £200. 30 Florrie Lindley. 31 Linda – the baby was christened Paul. 32 Emily Nugent and Ernest Bishop. 33 May Hardman who lived with her daughter Christine when the series opened. 34 Post Office Supervisor. 35 She was Billy's landlady and Jack was paying the rent. 36 Bessie Street School. 37 Lady Bracknell. 38 She poured a pint of beer over his head. 39 Alan Howard. 40 (b) Billy Nelson. 41 Leonard Swindley. 42 Joan Walker, daughter of Annie and Jack at the Rovers Return. 43 It was stolen by thieves. 44 Brian Tilsley. 45 Newton and Ridley. 46 The Glad Tidings Mission, Ena was the caretaker. 47 (c) Gail's pregnancy. 48 Ernest and Emily Bishop. 49 On the coach trip to Blackpool in 1961. 50 (c) Bet's shoe.

51 He collapsed and died at the wheel. 52 Hilda Ogden. 53 Baby linen. 54 Blanche Hunt, Deirdre's mum. 55 (c) A camping holiday. 56 Benny Lewis. 57 Monkey Gibbon. 58 Ernest Bishop. 59 Betty Turpin, Maggie's sister. 60 No one offered, so she paid it herself. 61 Valerie Tatlock. 62 Brian was a Catholic – Gail was not. 63 Bet Lynch. 64 (b) Kath Goodwin. 65 Eddie Yeats. 66 Vera Lomax. 67 In a road accident beneath the wheels of a bus. 68 An Italian restaurant. 69 With miners' lamps and clogs. 70 Because he faced a court case and possible bankruptcy over unpaid VAT. 71 Valerie Barlow, Ken's first wife. 72 (c) Liverpool. 73 Annie Walker. 74 (b) Syd Kippax. 75 Friday 9 December 1960 at 7 p.m.

76 Fred's Folly. 77 (c) Curly Watts and Elaine Pollard. 78 Military Medal. 79 Ernest Bishop. 80 Harry Bailey. 81 Stan Ogden. 82 Mavis' driving instructor caught decorator Dick Lewis changing before going to the theatre. 83 (c) No TV licence. 84 Brett Falcon. 85 Frank Barlow. 86 His taxi had a flat tyre. 87 Emily Nugent. 88 A mechanic at the Blue Bell Garage. 89 Hilda on her first day as his cleaner. 90 Harry, Concepta and Lucille Hewitt. 91 Intemperance – she was caught with a milk stout in the Rovers. 92 Lucille Hewitt. 93 GPO Supervisor. 94 Ena Sharples. 95 University librarian. 96 Thirty-five gold sovereigns. 97 HMS Andrew. 98 Ena Sharples. 99 Amalgamated Steel, Weatherfield. 100 The Orinoco Club.

'Not a word too many. Not a gesture needless. It is the best writing and acting I could wish to see . . .'

SIR JOHN BETJEMAN